Dance the SELF Free

& Live Your Best Life!

By Leianna Love

Dedication

To my beloved Mother,
Daughter and God!
Without you,
I would not exist.

Theresa -
Keep following
your Body.
Leionnae

Gratitudes

Everyone, everywhere, with whom I
have danced with to allow my life to
develop and blossom through the deep
connections of
love, laughter, fluidity and magic.
To all the teachers of
Ecstatic Conscious Dance,
you have moved me in more
ways than you know!
To friends and family who have
believed in me and helped me get this
book finished!
To Naropa University for an incredible
foundation to life!
Kiesa Kay for your incredible
additions to the work.
To Greg Dingizian and friends for believing in me and
showing me a path to success!
Chris Koehler for your fabulous "Burner" self
and edit support.
Victoria Bulostin for the last push.
You all Rock!
To Joan Marie for the Blue eyed owl!
To Laura Lynne Dyer,
Tree House Wise Woman,
for the Magic Land Experience!
Jada Sunshine & Dennis O' Keefe
for the photos!

Table of Contents

Introduction

Growing into the Practice

Outcomes of the Practice

Unique Dances
Holding Space
Embodiment
Mindfulness
Compassion
Expansion
Being Seen
Seeing Others
The Shine of the Inner Crystal

The Advanced Practice

Trance State
The Energy Orgasm
Tantric Dance
Self Care is Word

Totality

Introduction

For years, I have been led to write a book, but couldn't put a finger on what. As I was dancing down a street in Denver CO one day, my mind was busy searching for the answer to this particular question. Suddenly, there it was: Dance! Of course!

As a natural mover and a graduate from Somatic Dance Therapy this answer made complete sense. I have danced more dances than you can imagine. Initially, it was to find comfort in the world; secondly, it was to find my inner strength and grow; and lastly, it was to connect to others.

I have been working and traveling the last 5 years, therefore my dancing self has slowed down. Thankfully, it has given me the time to write this book, share with you great insights, and start you on a positive journey to self development.

It is my utmost desire to assist you on a path to self-expression and development. I'm aware not everyone dances, or feels comfortable doing so, but if you are a human, you move no matter what; you walk, you run, you do yoga. Whatever your path, these teachings will enable you to look deeper within your psyche, your heart and your mind.

It is my pleasure to introduce you to free form conscious dance. It is where we remove the obstacles that lay before us: cell phones, computers, earbuds, reluctance, discomfort and illusions and instead take notice of ourselves, and one another, allowing our bodies to feel the music and connect deeply with hearts of like-enjoyment. Let's remember what it means to live in and among community; let's laugh, be silly, and be in touch once again.

--The Journey begins Now!

People from all walks of life choose to participate in some form of community dance because it means finding a creative way to:

****

*Express feelings
*Grow more deeply
*Disconnect from binds that hold feelings hostage.
*Share deep experiences with others.
*Be supported in personal growth.

Invitation

A Gold Rush once drew explorers from many lands, but now the gold we need shines deep within us. We no longer have to cross oceans or travel in covered wagons across vast territories. We no longer have to take a rocket to the stars. The new frontier lives within. All we need is to do is look inside. Being an explorer now means traveling inward, not outward, and settling into acceptance of our strength. True adventure awaits us in our own unexplored caverns.

You can begin this journey inward to Self now. Let this book be your guide. You, too, will become a dancer of spirit and an explorer of Self.

By opening this book, you have chosen to join an enormous surge of proactive adults, diving deep to journey home. Welcome to this guidebook, an offering from my higher spirit to yours. May you become who you were born to be, both in everyday life and on every dance floor. Are you ready to play, become curious, laugh, love, weep, and drink deeply of Joy? Then let's start dancing.

Dance Freely

To nurture this true essence of contentment and dance along the pathway of free expression, you simply need to release the obstacles that have been placed between your all-knowing inner wisdom and your free-flowing spirit. Your individualized, authentic nature knows how to dance. The unencumbered flow of Self relates to this world with ease and grace of continuous movement, with no need for instruction.

Many pathways can feed the Soul's need for expression. We can make love or make music, paint murals or choose tattoos, whisper or shout. This book offers one pathway and will support you in learning how to move freely in body, mind, and spirit through the art of free form, ecstatic dance. In all the changing tides of life, we will lose homes, lovers, friends, pets, possessions, and all things familiar. Whatever happens to us, though, we will live in our bodies all of our lives. As those bodies change and grow, we can deepen connection to Spirit through the changes. Finding the natural ebb and flow of body and Spirit on the dance floor intensifies the pleasure in the ebb and flow of life.

We were born to dance freely. Before anyone imposed a vision on who or how we ought to be, we knew how to breathe, to move, and to feel. To dance freely means to get beneath the constructs, concepts, teachings and beliefs imposed upon us by other people's expectations, and to lift those false images up and out of our body to empower ourselves to be fully alive, fully present, and fully expressive in the moment. Deep inside, we already know how to dance freely, but these societal expectations and life's hardships block the portals of pleasure. We have an inherent ability to enjoy natural movement. Free expressions exists innately. We know instinctively how to cuddle, crawl, play, and walk. We know how to reach for each other, hold hands, kiss, and stretch into glorious days and nights of lovemaking. We feel the call to be free, but demands from others can smother that feeling. The time has come, right here and right now, to release all the old restrictions.

Have you ever watched a baby discover his or her own feet, hands, learning to taste, to touch, to feel? Let's reconnect with that sense of discovery, that curiosity about ourselves. Be ready to expand your authentic presence. Have courage.

Claim Self as a Free Spirit

I do a double-take whenever I am called a free spirit, because aren't we all, after all, free spirits? Since when did a free spirit become something extraordinary? As David Whyte says, "The world was meant for you to be free in . . . . Anything that does not set you free . . . is too small for you."

When did thinking for yourself, asking questions, finding your own way, and creating your own life make you different from others? Following a prepared path well-trodden by others never needs to become anyone's norm. The homogeneity and acceptance code that puts monetary success above spiritual development has taken its toll on our lives and our world. Conformity brings a false sense of belonging, identity, and safety. With the development of a true self-concept, the need to conform falls away. In some parts of American society, standing out can be a real no-no. The tall poppies get cut short to look the same as all the others. Success becomes a matter of subconscious messaging to conform.

To be accepted in some groups, it becomes mandatory to dress like others in the group, drive the same vehicle, have the same type of house, go to the same restaurants, and even feel the same, flat-line feelings – with a modest bandwidth of emotion extending from modest and pleasant, to content and happy. Otherwise, the group asserts harsh judgements. Next time you are in a public place, take a moment to take the social temperature of the cultural climate. Is there deviation among the people around you? Is this difference celebrated, ignored, or shunned entirely? How do you respond, and do you feel comfortable expressing yourself in the group? If not, perhaps you need to find or create a new group, where awareness, deep feelings, and self-expression have a home.

Ponder a bit about the people in your life who truly stand out as individuals. Do you like the difference, or do you judge them for being different? Does the difference affect your life or your appreciation for life in any way? What foods, entertainment, and housing preferences do your friends share, and is there homogeneity in the groups you frequent? Do you feel you have an edge on being a bit different from your peer group, and what is your personal comfort level with people who think, act, dress, speak, or move differently from you?

Imagine, too, what a visitor from another planet might think, seeing diverse people striving to be the same in a given environment. Where is the individuality in your place of work, in your home, or in your recreational activities? Consider neighborhood covenants, dress codes, employee policies, and public laws. At what point do these conformities stop being a means to keep order in a civilized nation, and become an infringement on personal liberty and self-expression? Where do you set your boundaries or draw your lines?

Product consistency can lead to an end to diversity. If fast food needs to taste the same in any country, then the individual flavors of each region won't be part of that multicultural menu. Factories need to churn out the same products again and again, and one individual's desire to make an improvement will be overridden by that drive for consistency across the board.

In America, it begins well before entry to the workforce. Individuality in school settings often gets crushed to dust. The school systems require conformity as a means to control large groups, and teachers striving to teach state standards and tests can become frustrated with the lack of ability to express that inner fire and passion for teaching. Students, forced to crunch their bodies into uncomfortable desks for hours at a time, can become miserable. Following rules with no consciousness of self can destroy spirit. The smallest difference in garments, reading material, or language usage can become a point of criticism, too often giving rise to shame or condemnation, instead of mutual understanding and celebration of difference.

We live in an overpopulated world, and the labels of right, wrong, and acceptable sometimes rob individuals of the human right to be and feel real. To play, to dance, and to dream become imperative for the survival of our souls.

The greatest changes, innovations, and inventions in our world often come from minds that think differently and simply can't conform to what others say to think, do, or be. The call of truth beckons with such a clamor that conformity to anything besides that inner vision, that inner whisper simply becomes impossible. Examples abound. Galileo insisted that the world was round, and he got imprisoned for his free thinking. The artist Vincent Van Gogh sold only one painting in his lifetime. Emily Dickinson saw only seven of her poems published and had no idea that anyone would value her work. Bill Gates, co-founder of Microsoft, dropped out of Harvard. And yet, these unique beings, in their difference, have been beacons of light for multiple seekers whose lives have been enriched by their creativity, by their true colors, shining. When we dance ourselves free, we release any need to look or move like other people around us. We listen and move to the guidance of our own inner light.

As a society, we may be missing incredible new developments and insights by marginalizing and rejecting people who think differently from ourselves. Sometimes people attain mental health labels when they simply have profound information waiting to be shared with others.

Strangeness can be beautiful, and need not be dangerous. As Emily Dickinson wrote, "Much Madness is Divinest Sense, to a discerning eye; much sense, divinest madness. Tis the majority. In this, as all prevail. Assent, and you are sane. Dissent, and you are dangerous, and handled with a chain." If we agree with the majority, if we blend, then we reap the benefits of inclusion. When we stand up, stand out, and move forward, we sometimes risk exclusion, until we find those others who will move forward with us. Ecstatic dancers develop kinesthetic (embodied) intelligence and the ability to feel the invisible vibrations that link us all.

People identified as strange by their peers often have more intensity and insight than the people who like to give those labels. Not every person can be productive all the time, and most people need a time of contemplation, quietude, and silence to create anything truly original. Color, intelligence, and humor emerge most freely from people allowed time to feel feelings, think originally, and dance. Some people truly cannot live within the confines of a traditional 40-hour work week, or a life of weekends and a two-week vacation a year. If we are lucky, we have someone in our lives who can conform well enough to keep us afloat, or we can find ways of living on the edge that allow us to keep a modicum of dignity. Sometimes simple survival depends upon knitting together several part-time jobs. Whatever we do for a living does not need to define who we are. Every human being has something to teach, and something to learn. The normalcy myth can become a tool we use to beat our own creative fire into submissive embers. The problem won't be that others douse our flames, but that we, ourselves, internalize the shaming and begin to erase our greatest gifts in order to conform.

That beautiful soul-pumping machine called your body can shake you loose, turn you inside out, and bring you home to your truest individuality. The dance floor is the place to begin becoming totally yourself, separate and apart from all external judgements and feel completely safe eventually. With community dance, you can find your own self-concept, step out on your own, learn to listen, and move to the rhythm of your own heartbeat.

The dance floor can be the best place to check into your own free spirit. If we really felt into our truest selves, we all would feel freedom deep inside. Many cultures incorporate Dance into spiritual practice. Hasidic Jews dance, and during Simchat Torah, it's a mitzvah, or good deed, to dance and celebrate. Wiccans do countless dances to heal the Earth, including the amazing Spiral Dance popularized by Starhawk. Sufis dance joyfully, and the whirling dervishes sometimes seem to embody the circular orbits of spinning planets.

I see many people searching for something with more meaning in everyday life. Many people simply do not know where to turn to release the doldrums of everyday reality and how to truly connect with another human being. Dancing in community awakens us, giving us permission to step out of the grip of normalcy and shakes up our reality as we deepen and explore undiscovered places in the psyche.

So take a moment now. Where is your strength? Where is your individuality, and how do you find it? Has there been any time in your life when you've identified as a free spirit, an outsider, or a stranger? Consider if a calamity transpired, and you became completely alone, with no family connections and no community to comfort you. On your own, with no one but yourself to please, what would you choose to do? How would you survive? Does your fear of being homeless, being different, or being hurt keep you from exploring your own edge, or stop you from taking risks? What fear stops you, and what comforts feed you?

A Personal Quest for Freedom

Dancing always has been and will be my truest path to enjoying the life I was born to live. Dancing my own dance set me from the binds of my mind that held me back from my authentic nature.

As a young girl, each time I had the chance to dance my own way, I loved it! I eventually got a glimpse of something greater than the persona I carried or what society labeled me to be. I glimpsed something deeper – connection to my Spirit. Dancing authentically helped me grow into the me I longed to be! The dance floor became an oasis of personal freedom, and I learned that any floor can become a dance floor – be it the soft sands of a beach on Maui, a forest floor in the Appalachians, or the bamboo floor at a friend's retreat.

As a child, my family's religion frowned on dancing. I got good grounding and a connection to spiritual values through my Southern Baptist heritage, but the religion of my youth had disdain for my own greatest source of power. Can you imagine? As a little dancer spirit who loved to move, play, and express through dance, I found myself deemed a misfit, admonished not to dance as it could awaken evil spirits.

My own experience has shown me the opposite is true. Dancing protects me and lifts me up from all manner of harm. Dancing actually has been the free form of my own spiritual connection. If anything, it brings me closer to God, Spirit, and all that shines most purely within me.

I deeply love my family and respect their church and beliefs, and I respect them with all my heart. In childhood, the message came large that somehow my connection to dance meant that I had a diabolical side, and I even was told that dancing meant opening to being a child of the devil.

Imagine, for a moment, that you were born with certain talents, and an innate sense of goodness that countered everything you had been taught to believe about Spirit from your family of origin. If you have had any of these messages given to you, take a moment, right now, to wash yourself clean of these wrong-headed misconceptions. Fearing what gives us deepest power and strength only diminishes us. Never believe that you might be wrong, because that gene or quality that differentiates you from your milieu could be burnished into something bright and beautiful within you. We will celebrate your dancing spirit, and make sure it will not be extinguished by ignorance or criticism.

My own journey took many years of therapy, and training to become a therapist myself. I can say, with certainty, that telling a child who is naturally good at something, a child who feels good doing something beautiful, that the behavior somehow is strange or wrong, can destabilize the connection between Self and Spirit. If your journey home has been a long one, as mine has been, then I offer you a moment of pure encouragement. All of us need support to develop those qualities that gleam most brightly, most fully alive, within us.

My family may have disapproved, but I needed to dance. Dancing kept me alive. I have felt a sense of aliveness and my deepest connection to God in my dancing. I also maintain a deep connection to those roots and that heritage. My forebears and I share an unflinching belief in the divine, and in something greater than what we see in everyday life. The poet Dylan Thomas called it "the force that through the green shoot drives the flower," and each one of us can reach and revitalize that force within ourselves.

Dancing got me through some very tough times. I found a familiar, safe place where I could go, a place that was truly mine. I understood and trusted this inner haven. Through the expression and creative art of dance, I felt in my heart that I belonged somewhere in this world. Growing up can be difficult, and we find strategies that work: mine happened to be expressive dance, and it still is.

So take a moment, as you reflect on my journey, to consider what obstacles you have internalized about allowing yourself the freedom to dance. Have you, like me, felt insecure, or judged yourself? Have you feared your own power, or worried about what other people may think of you?

Some of us have dance studios and lessons available, and supportive families. Even with that support for the physical dance, we might be pushed into dancing with certain steps or styles, with no freedom of expression. Since I had no lessons, my dancing emerged completely free. I had no one to guide me, so I could rely entirely on my inner guidance, doing what felt the best.

Dancing happens in so many ways in our blended American culture, and I found a way to follow my drive for self-expression by joining the cheerleading squad so I could do dance routines with others. I also organized a dance squad in high school, and it quickly became the happiest time of all my school years. I still remember the squad "Rhapsody in Blue." We were so dynamic! Youth and energy emboldened us. This success led me to choose physical education as a bachelor's degree, and dance movement therapy became my path in graduate school. Dancers dance.

My path never gave me simple steps toward being a dancer, but the personal journey of self-development that resulted from overcoming obstacles, gave me a deep insight that I want to share with you. The little girl who hid to dance has grown up to be a guide for you, so you can free yourself to dance along your own life's path.

It took me many years to set myself free from a belief system that denigrated my own greatest gifts. Being a professional dancer on stage did not become my calling, but dancing my way to personal freedom and sharing that knowledge has become essential to everyday life. I was lucky enough, as a young girl, to learn and teach actual steps at Arthur Murray Dance Studio. Now I offer you the stepping stones that will lighten your life as a free form dancer.

Along the way, I learned not to believe everything others say, to trust and love that inner spark within the Self, and to settle for nothing less than a personal connection to Spirit. Once you declare dance as your spiritual path and path to wellness, your life will begin to open and change as the flow of energy that you embrace becomes an energy stream you can use.

My Boots

My boots have seen a lot of Earth

Miles and miles to be exact

Of places unknown…

Traveled, hiked, danced and loved,

Finding my way through it all.

Like a fairy fluttering

Never knowing quite where to land

Getting caught in the cage called life.

I sit…I ponder…I worry…to the point of picking up and leaving…walking, …again…to a new territory…singing the song of sweet sorrows… hearing melodic tunes of days gone by.

Trapped is unkind,

Bondage is terrifying,

Breaking loose…always…my boots.

Vibrations of the Hearing Impaired

Not being able to hear the way most people hear has been both a great obstacle and a great blessing in my life. From an early age, I could not detect the auditory signals that others heard, so I learned to rely on other signs, sights, and intuitions. I couldn't say certain words, like sugar, and a speech therapist worked with me.

My ears did not work like everyone else's ears, and so my brain didn't conform, either. I couldn't join the banter in group settings, but learned to focus and absorb as much connection and information as possible one-on-one. I could feel the vibrations and sense the shifting moods, but I could not rely on any sounds to guide me.

Spoken rules and directions slid past me, so I had to try with all my might to figure out what people needed or wanted from me by paying extra careful attention to their feelings and responses to all I did. I learned to watch carefully, and to feel things unspoken. Early on in school, I sat in the front row whenever I could, because otherwise I simply could not absorb any of the intended lessons.

After high school graduation, I applied to go into the Air Force. Going all the way through to the testing for recruitment, the recruiter said there would definitely be jobs that I would never perform due to my hearing loss. I was only 19 at the time, so many years, still awkward in company of others; still wondering why I was so different; wondering why I did not belong. Years continued to go by and my only true connection, my best form of interpersonal communication, became dance. I could lose myself to the vibration of the music.

The vibration of sound took me far away into my body and out of my struggle. It was me and the music- the deep base, the lyrical flute, the heart-opening drumbeat of sound. I could not tell you the words. My idea of what the words might be could result in hilarity, but my feel for the rhythms and pulsations of the music never failed me.

I did not know in youth that being hard of hearing would lead me to a fulfilled life as a healer, listening to the vibrations of others' energy. I learned instinctively how to tune into a different channel to receive information. I have learned through my loss and my struggles how to connect in an entirely different way, with no words.

My experience, growing up almost entirely deaf, was that I did not belong in the auditory world, orchestrated to be understood fully by all who can hear! People who process through their ears can join in conversations, being quick-witted, sarcastic, and able to slice with their verbal acuity.

My way took more time, more patience; I knew early that I never would be a hearing person, able to make fast decisions while talking through troubles. My kinesthetic gifts soared, but my auditory ability sunk to subterranean depths. To understand others, I learned to listen deeply without using my ears.

I never knew how much life I missed out on and why I was as paranoid as I was as a young person, until I got my first pair of hearing aids. Holy cow! My life changed! Suddenly, I could hear the traffic, yes, even the car behind me in the parking lot. I appeared friendlier, more engaged and open in interactions. My daughter used to answer for me so I wouldn't look anti-social, and suddenly I heard when others spoke, and could answer for myself. From my teen years until I reached the age of 35, I lived in a completely different zone. I never knew how hearing loss might have been a root cause of my clumsiness in social situations, my inability to understand the things others seemed to perceive with ease. I thought it was just me, born strange, different, my drum beating entirely to a different drum that no one else heard! I was alone, sad, depressed, and angry. I couldn't hear birds sing.

I also had developed sensitivity to the unspoken,

nonverbal communication that others often miss or ignore. I became gratified, even overjoyed, to learn that there are people like me. They like what I have to say and they enjoy the ability to banter with me. Yes. I enjoy it, too. I am grateful every single day for my hearing aids, my new ears, as I call them. Yes, I was given hearing devices that changed my world! For years, friends had urged me to get my hearing checked, but I simply refused; I did not know what I was missing.

In 2016, I ventured to Bali, and the healing from that long time of disorientation reached its apex. I was given a gift of an incredible healer to heal the deep seated wounding of my child, young adult years. Yes, I had my ears, but for years I was still walking around with intense wounding from the years that preceded the change. These wounds were still running the show. The issue of not belonging or being able to banter at a dinner party with grace and ease was still inside of my being, as was the belief that I could not engage intellectually with three or more people at once. Even though I could hear, I still did not know how to relate in an audio world, because I never learned. What I learned was how to read energy, lips, body language, subtle changes in frequencies, facial expressions, and self-expressive dance! The wounding inside of me remained hidden but deeply present for more than a decade. I never thought anyone could heal my hearing, but the real healing came from releasing the beliefs around my hearing that held me hostage for years.

In Bali and with the help of two amazing people, I visited a strong, quiet man who wanted no attention for himself as he channeled an Old Woman. She rubbed my skin with her fingers and drew the wounding to the surface. It hurt! I wanted to run, but knew something was real. I have never felt anything so intense besides childbirth, but I tell you, the well of sorrow that burst through me was so, so deep! I could not believe it! And for days after I wrote, reflected, and celebrated!

I was free from this nasty belief that I was different and somehow not good enough to be normal. I am more than normal. We all have super powers, and they often come from the same source as the wounds. In nature, the source of pain is often close by. For example, when poison ivy rings a tree, the jewelweed that will remove the sting of that ivy often grows beside it. In my life, the hearing loss meant that I could not interact with the kind of ease that my peers took for granted, but I found a deep source of connection that did not rely on the audio.

What I realize now after this healing is that our everyday world often does not make room for people who are different and have a different learning channel. If you don't hear, you may not even know what you're missing. There are not subtitles on a major motion picture. You have to stand out and ask for those silly headphones in order to enjoy the movie. You see, as a hearing impaired person I have developed the ability to read those subtitles and watch the movie without hesitation. You would, too, if necessary. More than likely, however, you can hear, and may never have had to tap into a different part of your brain. My survival depended on accessing an unusual avenue, and after a time of struggle, that difficulty has revealed its hidden blessing.

A hearing loss is an invisible disability, unseen but clearly there. I have had friends in the past, close friends, who would get angry with me because I couldn't hear and they had to speak up. My response was and is, imagine I was in a wheelchair and you had to push me as we walked together; would you get angry?

I do not resent my hearing loss or others who do not understand. The loss resulted in amazing gains and many gifts beyond my imagination. It has led me into the most amazing dances, taught me how to communicate through dance, and led me to understand dance at a level very few will ever know. It also led me to be a dynamic dancer in my own right as an expressionistic mover. My difference, once perceived as a weakness, has become my strength, as I move to the vibrations and pulsations of others moving around me.

Growing into the Practice

Do Your Research

Many communities offer a form of community dance. These gatherings may bear many labels, including Ecstatic Dance, Azul, 5 Rhythms, Soul Motion, Open Floor, Beach Dance, or Dancing Freedom. As the dancing subculture develops and grows, we see individuals and communities form diverse dancing venues and collectives. The community members take the lead, establishing outlines and structures to bring people together in dancing harmony.

People everywhere are enjoying this free form phenomenon. The awakening of this awareness of the pleasures of free form dancing in groups seems timed to coincide with awakening and transitions needed in the world for our continual progress as a surviving species. The new venues support the mass awakening of Spirit by offering safe places to question and explore reality. Personal existence and meaning become the beginning of a great transition of mankind toward a more loving and connected reality.

Do an Internet search for Ecstatic or Conscious Dance. If you cannot find a collective or a community dance venue in your area, the nearest big town might have one. Festivals, too, sometimes feature community dances. Better yet, choose a teacher, and invite that teacher to visit your community to offer one of the most fun, lively experiential community gatherings you ever will experience.

Choose Your Venue:

- Is it ecstatic, 5 rhythms, soul motion, spiritual, or therapeutic?
- Does the community dance together often? Is there a facilitator to hold the space?
- Is it a well-known DJ? Is it a party?
- Is personal sharing part of the process?
- Is it loose or connected?

Visiting for the First Time

Dancing will support your greatest good. You will find that it improves your health, your relationships, your flexibility, and your overall well-being, so let's get you started on this journey with a few guidelines.

Talk with the teacher or facilitator. Contact the teacher or group facilitator beforehand if possible. A phone call or email will suffice. Share that the experience will be your first time in a community gathering of ecstatic and expressive dancers. Ask what the norms or rules of the group might be, and what guidelines you need to know before you begin. The teacher will offer insight and support to put you at ease.

As you enter the practice, do so with respect both to yourself and your fellow dancers, maintaining an attitude of sanctity and honor to the group, the teacher, and yourself. This will strengthen the experience of the journey.

Take notice of any implicit or explicit norms or rules. Is it quiet? Is it chatty? Are they barefoot or have shoes on? How is everyone dressed? These little things can say much about a group. Pay attention and it will be much easier to blend your energies with the existing group dynamic.

Once you enter the room, notice the level of physical closeness among certain dancers. The core of the dancing body very often will consist of the friends who have been dancing together for a long while. You too can have this depth of relating in time, as long as you keep dancing your own dance. Invite a friend along with you for the first time if this puts you at ease.

You may feel a bit intimidated at first, and it is completely normal to feel a bit outside of the group. You might want to go slowly, entering the group at the edges, feeling your way with caution or you may want to dive right into the dynamic, with group acceptance as your goal.

Check in with yourself and study your response with healthy curiosity, no judgement needed. Remember, too, no matter where you are on this first day, ease into the room, being with only yourself first, giving yourself ample time to drop into your body and then into the moving, active group. Stay with yourself, your feelings, and very own journey.

More than likely, the group has a warm up phase in which you can simply enter without talking to anyone. Once you are inside, find a place that feels good to you. Look for an opening in the room that feels safe, comfortable, and fitting for where and how you feel in the moment. Most beginners tend to gravitate to the periphery (outside) of the room instead of the middle, but go where you feel most at ease.

If you feel comfortable and you are in the right space, kiss the floor with your body! Meaning, make contact with the floor. Get down on your knees, and then your behind, and lay down! Allow your body to become one with the floor. The floor is the best place to truly feel what is happening inside of you. We habitually stand every day! Standing is simple, and lying on the floor may be more challenging. So getting out of old habits is the first rule of truly experiencing something new and the key to letting go. Try it! Stand if you must, but once you have the courage to explore the floor, it will move you in ways you never thought possible.

Close your eyes and feel the room, the pulse, the rhythm, the energy. Notice yourself again, and take your emotional temperature. Where are you? What do you feel inside? Maybe your heart is beating, maybe your mouth is dry, or maybe your palms are sweaty. Great! Body based experiences happen best when we explore new places and pathways.

If you feel your emotions emerge, like sadness, anger, and frustration, refrain from judgment. I will say it again. Do not judge yourself! Refrain from self-criticism, too! This type of mind-tripping only makes what can be joyful turn into something painful. Yes, the mind often gets caught up in criticism, and sometimes wants to remind us of all the negative, shaming, self-blaming things that we dance away.

If these negative thoughts flow, try to stop them. If the mind begins chattering about how old or young we are, comparing our level of fitness with others or some idealized goal, do some thought-stopping practices. Take a deep breath, become aware of your thoughts and try to redirect to what you are feeling instead. Now, dance freely, and let your inner dialogue reflect the flow and freedom of the moment, without judgement. Stay with the present experience. Live the moment.

To ground and center in the space, take notice of what your five senses tell you. What do you see, hear, taste, touch, smell? Allow yourself to experience the moment with no harshness. Now, notice the beauty around you, hear the music, be in the room, and take a deep breath.

In a safe space with your eyes closed, breathe! Dancing freely means inhaling deeply. While breathing, take notice of the kind of breath you are inhaling. Is it shallow? Is it quick? Is it random? We all habitually have a pattern of breathing and until we take notice of the pattern we will continue to inhibit our greatest vitality, because a habituated life force is exactly that, habitual, set, familiar, old groove playing the same old story. We begin to change the story by being present in the mind and conscious of the breath.

Practice opening and closing your eyes. Be Out and then In! Out means you are aware of that which is happening outside yourself. It means being aware of inner workings, sensations, feelings, and aches and pains.

When we move our attention to different aspects of Self, or our environment, we're practicing what dance therapists call oscillation. Oscillate with the polarities that are present. The In closes inside you, and the Out opens to all around you.

As the music shifts to an upbeat rhythm, the vibration invites you to move faster, outward. Generally the initial music is deep and slow and encourages you to drop into your body slowly and with ease, warming your muscles and your nerves. The music then quickens, paced to follow your own natural rhythm of movement. This universal rhythm supports your body's natural way in any kind of exercise. We start out gently, get more vigorous, then highly charged, and finally relax deeply.

The music may shift again, inviting more energy. Remember the outside of the dancing group, the periphery, is generally where newcomers begin. As a newcomer simply explore the room first, moving around, practicing the In/Out exercise as I mentioned earlier, feeling the room and the energies, and feeling your feelings. Instead of closing your eyes completely, stand tall and simply downcast them standing with your eyes half closed, not fully shut but simply relaxed to ensure that you are aware of others dancing in the room, especially the ones next to you.

While experiencing this new space, it's important to stay safe and awake in all the senses while dancing with many different energies and people at the same time.

When you feel ready, expand into the space. Dancing a full-on dance means being aware of smell, touch, sight, taste, and sound all at once, and being able to engulf the whole room in a moment. Feel the energetic waves all around you. There may be ten or more other people moving at all different speeds and with all kinds of expressions right next to you. Breathe into the energy field. Feel the rhythm of your new friends as they dance their individual expression of life in the moment.

Tune in and feel what sadness smells like, hear the sound of someone expressing joy, taste the memory someone is having, see the essence of the human spirit alive. We can open the sensory channels at any given moment when we bring our attention to them.

The practice of free form dance reminds us to notice our senses and bring them to our full attention. Learning to tune into the sensory channels during the practice expands into a great practice for being in the everyday world, since oftentimes, we get caught up in the focused, narrow channels of productivity and forget to expand ourselves outwardly to the field of consciousness. Once we become fully aware of the sensory channels, we realize we can breathe in the scent of the trees and the fresh air, and constantly remind ourselves of the interconnectedness of all things, and what is really important in life. We practice the subtle joy of being awakened to the moment. We begin to notice the scent of blooming roses, the sound of raindrops on a tin roof, and the softness of a puppy's fur. Give yourself permission to slowly unfold into your own organic flower.

Engaging in free style dance for the first time is both invigorating and intimidating. It brings "things" up that you may have become numb to in your everyday existence. Give it time, go slowly, follow your own guidepost to your own comfort. There is no rush here. I promise you, given enough time and practice, you will emerge into a realm so profound, your life will change for the better.

The Different Venues

Two main venues of free form dance deserve differentiation: community dances and raves. Community dances are those that are set up as a gathering of people who dance together on a regular basis and grow individually and together at the same time. New members drop in randomly. These groups may meet two to three times a week, and the hope is that they grow into love and make space for deeper emotional experiences because of the trust and safety that has been established among the dancers.

On the opposite end of the spectrum, you'll find Rave dances that host DJs and spin amazing Galactic tunes. Dancers generally are in their own head space and occasionally tend to space out on whatever social drug might be in reach. The raves feel more like night clubs, although they have more physical intimacy and group cohesion than the traditional bar scene. You are not as apt to be held close by other dancers or by the space because this venue is primarily a loose group with no facilitation or leader besides the one choosing the tunes.

I encourage anyone new to this art to check out a few different offerings available to you, and then decide what feels the best, and what your desire is from the experience. Then you will be on your way.

Find the Courage to Play

Courage is the catalyst into the unknown. Exploring your individualized Self as a free dancer takes more than a fun, safe atmosphere. It takes courage, as well, which I have hinted to so far. Dancing freely takes courage because dancing your own dance means no one is going to show you how. What a beautiful metaphor this is for life itself.

You can stand on the sidelines and look at your life at any time, bemoaning how it is not working or what is wrong with it. How one approaches their world in times of struggle, loss, transition or opportunity can be guidepost to the innermost source of resilience and strength. Change begins, however, when we decide to jump in fully and allow the unknown to emerge. Your deepest desire to find meaning becomes the first, most essential ingredient to the possibility of finding it.

Life is not our own as long as someone else controls us or shoves us along the path, so we become what others want us to be. Many people are confused as adults because of the impressions made upon them by their own parents. Supportive parents help us to become the best person possible, but within the confines and constructs of what they understand to be true, and what is comfortable for them. They use their tools, resources, beliefs and experiences because this is all they have.

Now, it is up to us to question those constructs and teachings, and to begin to walk the lonely path of finding what is true and real for us as individuals, not the daughter or son of our parents, not as the husband or wife or lover of another, and not as the parent or grandparent of children who needs us to stay in a single role to fulfill their needs. We must be free to be who we need to be.

True Self emerges as we find the courage to take the journey, break through the obstacles, and face whatever is waiting to be discovered and uncovered in the subconscious mind. True power to grow and evolve dissolves or implodes when we give our power away to others or stay in the conditioning of our upbringing. Breaking free from these conditions in psychotherapeutic terms is referred to as individuation. We must individuate to truly come home to Self.

Maybe the fear of this individuating process is why some people choose to have a secure but unfulfilling job, or marriage for that matter. Facing the wounds, vulnerabilities, or unknowns feels too scary. Sometimes we have times when we feel we must sacrifice self-fulfillment for certain kinds of security, or to support the ones we love through challenging times. Pretending all is well is a fabulous fallacy. Laziness lurks as we scheme for ways to lavish in the luxuries of life without getting uncomfortable!

In the world of free expression, life begins from the inner journey, the one that goes deep into the recesses of the undiscovered aspects of mind, body, and spirit. This depth never will be found from fallacy. Material possessions and the cravings for these goods create a false identity and tend to rob our truest nature from us. We trade inner peace for outer trappings of a successful material life, and soon we find ourselves trapped within a suffocating web. We work hard, earn money, buy things, set up a comfortable life, and never look inside our own hearts.

Electronic gadgets too often replace the true intimacy of touch, connection, and sharing our individual, inner wisdom. Prescription drugs appear as the answer to despair, insomnia, and loneliness in ads. The pressure to take pills to fix ourselves looms large. When we get curious and start asking questions, we enter dangerous territory, because as soon as we do we will certainly question the manifestation of this unhealed society. As long as we meander along the road of pretending, we will continue to inhibit the blossoming of the uniqueness and fullness that longs to unfold in this lifetime. Imagine the change on a large scale for this world, for the earth, if most of us who have been following the prescribed program to what we have been told is success, actually decided to do some inner work instead, and emphasize healing ourselves and the earth. How different our collective reality might be if we joined together. I like to imagine all meetings beginning with a brief dance, an antidote to all the talking.

I am not declaring that you should radically change your life, but I am supporting you to find the courage to attempt to get on a dance floor to begin the process of getting a tad uncomfortable with new experiences, hang out in the mystery of the unknown, and follow your own lead.

Dancing freely offers a way to bring your mind, soul, and body into alignment, so you can move more comfortably on the earth. Your own magnetic field will resonate with a new vibration when you begin dancing. Beyond the spectrum of what can be seen with the eyes, a new inner peace awaits to bloom within you. Dancers come to the realization that true alignment is where true wealth of body, mind and spirit begins. Continuing the practice of discovering new aspects of yourself in this manner will open a resurgence of your desire to bring more of this experience in your relationships, your employment, and your home. When you stretch to fill the corners of your emptiness and your prescribed programs, you may find an infinite light within yourself waiting to shine like none other.

Tune into the Rhythmic Body

Getting familiar with the body as an instrument of rhythm provides another vehicle to free expression. Our bodies can move with natural grace and ease if we simply let go. Like many things in our lives, however, we want to control the movements of our bodies to conform to the familiar. We control as many aspects of our lives and bodies as we can to feel safe, but this illusion of safety can hamper the natural flow of our own rhythms.

Learning to trust the rhythmic body takes time. Old habits work hard to run the show, even on the dance floor! We cannot create new results by repeating the same old mistakes or methods.

Lest we forget, learning new, natural, uninhibited movement needs nurturing and time. The body knows how to shake, swing, pulse, and surrender without instruction. The trouble is, we can get stuck in the same old mind-driven movement pattern that barely, if ever, changes rhythm.

Luckily, the moving body is the best place to notice how controlled we are in our lives. Your own body truly can be your greatest teacher. When beginning the practice of dancing your own dance, many people generally repeat the same movement pattern. The nervous system creates grooves, and it truly feels at ease going into the same groove every time. Dancing freely however, unlocks the old habits and expands the openness in the body, the mind, and all aspects of life!

The more familiar we become with freestyle movement, the easier to understand how much control is being exercised daily, inhibiting a natural flow to our life. The moving body is absolutely indicative of how we relate to life and others. Janet Adler, a founder of movement therapy, asks this question: "Are you moving your body, or is your body moving you?" Are you controlling your life or do you allow it to unfold? You see, it goes both ways. As we become more fluid and trusting in the body on the dance floor, we then enhance our own ability to shift our behavior with the outside world. The dance floor gives us information to how we relate to Self and those around us.

Long ago when I began the practice of ecstatic free-form, I was very comfortable dancing by myself. I took great comfort in going in, exploring, and enjoying myself, by myself. This inward focus was how I lived my life, single, solo, and filled with a humming contentment. Nowadays, I have shifted. I am more apt to be seen on the dance floor in relationship with others, creating amazing, in the moment, dances. In my life, I spend most of my time with others as well, creating and imagining all things possible.

You see, there is a direct parallel here. Our moving body truly has the potential to teach us how we relate to the world and with others. Dancing shows us where we hold tight and where we cling in the body and the mind and how this is evident in our relationships. Do we attach to outcomes? Hold tight to person with the fear they may leave us? Do we roam around the room meeting people's gaze? Do we stay on the sideline without ever greeting anyone? The free form practice is a tell tale sign on where our comfort lies in with others outside the dance floor.

When we choose the practice of dancing freely we make a decision to crack the mold and break free of old habits. The mold that has held us together in the identity, the persona, and the old habits that no longer serve our deepest authentic selves. You see, cracking the mold comes from allowing the body to move you; not you moving your body. We decide consciously to get our minds out of the driver's seat and trust that something greater than our mind knows the way. Only then, my friend, can a true sense of joy and radiance break through and shine outward. The radiance revealed through dancing freely becomes a bountiful source of light, love, and rainbows in our lives.

Witness your Sensations

You have the power to observe yourself in whatever you are participating in at any given moment, by learning to pay attention to your thoughts, your sensations, your body, and how your feelings flow and change accordingly. In somatic dance therapy we have a name for this objective observation: it is acting as our own Self Witness, and observing ourselves objectively in the moment. In daily life, it is easy to be unaware of what we are doing and feeling. Eating, talking, listening, walking, driving, texting-- all the things we do become a simple groove in the nervous system and we can ride through whatever we are doing without ever paying conscious attention to what is happening in the moment, or in the body, for that matter.

Achieving heightened awareness takes practice. Janet Adler, dance therapist and founder of Authentic Movement, teaches us how to become our own Self witness. She uses the terms mover and witness. The mover takes the position in the middle of the floor while the witness sits on the edge. There is no music, only awareness. The witness watches the mover and notices feelings on a somatic, or body-based level, by tuning into every gesture, expression, and attitude that changes in the mover. The witness stays without judgement or applying a story, only watching and tuning into their own sensations in the body. The Mover is in the space being witnessed by the observer, noticing on a somatic level the feeling, charges, nuances, arising in every moment as they freely express themselves being held with attention by the witness.

The development and premise of this application teaches us that we can acknowledge and be present with our own actions, thoughts, and interactions, and at the same time observing someone else.

Sensations are your body's clues to what it wants. When you are hungry, you get the sensation of growling in the stomach. When you are afraid, you might feel tight in the gut. All of these signs are information to the brain, alerting the brain that your body needs attention. Learning to listen more acutely to the messages and sensations can truly improve our relationships, careers, and status in the world. If we feel uncomfortable and can tune into this level of uncertainty, we will be more successful and healthier. We will know when it's time to go. Tuning into the body's sensation meter, we quickly detect a sore throat or something a bit off and hopefully tackle the bug early, before it settles too deeply. Using intuition, you can also sense when things simply don't feel quite right. Intuition is actually a felt sense in the body. A sort of knowing, ease, confirmation. We can pay careful attention to our alert signals as we become safe and familiar with them. Most of us, all too often, react quickly to a stimulus without ever really investigating the nature of it or the etiology of it. The art of bringing attention to what we feel and why, gives us valuable information for going deeper into our own Self development to understand and improve our reactivity.

You can begin to listen to finite shifts in the body as a free form dancer. Generally, it is a safe space to feel into your body and what it wants from you. Most familiar sensations include the emptiness in our belly when we are hungry, our rapid heartbeat when we are in a romantic exchange, or the pain in your rear when you have been writing too long. These are easy to grasp and understand. Sensations like the emptiness of abandonment; the energy that feels nervous and out of whack when you feel anxious; the intense pit of your stomach when you enter an unfamiliar space. These extreme sensations might be feelings we dodge or avoid, but by feeling them, we attain a deep level of knowledge about ourselves in relationship to others. Most of us have these sensations far more than we realize and do not have ways to process them or release them, therefore, we block, avoid, and dodge what's uncomfortable, creating a backlog of blocked emotions that create disease and discomfort in the body.

More pleasure can only be attained by working through what is stuck and held in the body. When we are blocked or numb, which many of us are, we can't even feel goodness or pleasure. Sometimes even pleasure is too intense. Once we become aware, move, give voice and recognition to these places begging for attention then we are on our way to a more full life.

Ode to Naked Feet

Oh the luxury of our feet naked on the earth.

Lush wet grass with mud oozing through our toes,

Squishy and sticky, sending tickling sensations up our spine.

Remembering ancestry of many lifetimes

As we parade as children.

Feeling self as the foot pushes off the ground from toes

That lead the movement.

Landing gently from the air, reaching for the unknown.

Softly caressing the foot of another,

Feeling the rough edges,

The smooth soles, the twinkling of toes dancing together.

Naked feet, always make me chuckle.

Dance on Naked Feet

In free style community dance, dancing barefoot is generally the norm. We dance this way for everyone's safety as a necessity since toes can be stepped on, legs are sometimes in the air, and shoes create noise. Being barefoot also brings us closer to the natural rhythms of the body because we are touching lightly against the earth. The feet are the sensors, the stabilizers, and the propellers of the dance.

In the next few moments, reconnect with those naked feet of yours. Take off your shoes. Wiggle your toes. Look at the shape of your foot. Don't judge your toenails, just appreciate them. Now stand up and feel the pads of your feet and the heel of your foot. Sink into the heaviness of you, and notice how your feet support you. If at any time as a dancer you feel disconnected, unglued or out of balance, bring awareness to your feet, feel the connection to the earth and the core of you connected to the ground.

Remember, too, to take care of yourself if you have issues with your feet. Wear jazz shoes or dancing slippers if you need them, or some light tennis shoes work as well. You can wear anything with soft soles and a small footprint.

Unfortunately, many people have grown distant from feeling feet against the naked earth. The lay of concrete floors, sidewalks, and foundations all demand soft cushioned shoes to be worn for support that the earth so naturally provided for years by itself. Sadly, we have begun to see and feel the damages to feet as well, as sore feet and fasciitis have become all too common these days. Concrete is rigid and unforgiving, which is what makes it valuable. However, when we dance or exercise on concrete floors we absorb the shock back into the bodies because concrete absorbs nothing. This jolt harms knees, joints, ligaments, and everything else. I can't for the life of me figure out why many movement spaces still have a concrete base. They may have a nice surface with a fancy wooden overlay, but dance on that baby and check in with your body the next day, and you will feel the results. Guaranteed, except if you are still quite young, your body is going to be unhappy.

Too many of our community dances and free movement exercises are still hosted on hard, unforgiving floors. I hope that we will awaken to the damages to our naked feet on this kind of surface and begin to take decisive action as a collective to change it. What we need is spring sprung or floating floors, which is what they are called.

If your space has a concrete floor, after you have established a connection to the group, you may want to share my proposal. Imagine if each dancer in any given group pitched in what they could afford toward a new, spring sprung floor that would outlast the dancing community into the communities of tomorrow. What a sweet gift or pay it forward action for future dancers!

I charge you, dear reader, to be the one who takes the initiative to organize a floor fund and embark on giving dancers yet to come, a bouncing, absorbing and loving floor, one that naked feet will love forever more.

The experience of Naked Feet against the earth is your birthright; let's not forget the luxury of this experience. Today, my friend, go for a walk in the park without shoes! Feel the earth, the mud, the dry grass, whatever lies beneath you, breathe in, relax, and let go.

Be in the Bubble

Engulfed in space electrified and charged, illuminating your light, protecting and shielding your personal expression of form and feelings, you find yourself surrounded by your own Dancing Bubble, the space that your body and energy occupy when moving. This bubble includes all the space that surrounds you when arms stretch wide, a leg kicks forward and the moving body surges!

You, and everyone else, have a personal dancing bubble. It is referred to as your kinesphere or boundary, and consists of the total amount of space you need to feel at ease.

We love our space. We especially love space on the dance floor and we want it to be respected and recognized for everyone participating in the community dance practice. This boundary, the healthy space between you and another, is essential to experiencing a successful dance. Beginners, in particular, can misconstrue the importance of the dancing bubble and violate space. I find it helpful as a free dancer to make it a habit not to touch someone from behind. For starters, they do not see you coming; and secondly, you don't have their permission. I cannot stress to you enough the importance of respecting this boundary in the dance. Dancers tend to go deep into their momentary bliss or abyss, where ever they are, it is imperative to respect this space. If this space is violated, some people may become frightened or angry from being taken by surprise. Community dance exists as a place of safe excitement, adrenaline from fun, not fear.

If you want to enter someone else's boundary make eye contact first, to check to see if they are inviting a dance with you or if they prefer being with themselves, in their own rhythm without external connection. The invitation of connection from eye contact can be taken or not, with no feeling of rejection or loss. Each person dances an individual, unique dance. For dancers turning inward, often eyes will be downcast or they will not make eye contact with you. Once eye contact is made, gently enter the moving space of the other dancer. Copy their movements, not necessarily as a mirrored reflection, but as a match to the rhythm and tone of the movement. For example, if one is pushing energy with their hands, maybe like beating a drum, the best way to join them is to beat a drum with your hands as well, mimicking their movement, but doing it your own way. Merging with someone this way signifies that you want to connect. You also convey your awareness, showing that you see them and are aware of their energy. By mirroring without mimicking, you can ease gently and quickly into the same energetic flow with the person or group you'd like to join.

The energetic boundary around our physical body is essential to good health. By developing this understanding it supports all of us to act a bit more slowly and mindfully when standing next to someone in conversation, movement or dancing. The dance floor feels as if everyone is just making love standing up, moving, which just might be the case, but staying conscious of your space and others will benefit the whole dance greatly. It keeps the fluidity and the safety in line so everyone can go deep or lose themselves, whatever the case may be.

Silence is Action

Community dance generally exists as a silent practice, so conversation occurs kinesthetically, through the body, where the study of ourselves in relationship can truly take place. Silent dancing simply means refraining from chatter or words. Then and only then are we granted the space to pay attention to thoughts, sensations, judgements, feelings, and ultimately the rhythm between ourselves and the other dancers.

Silent dancing also supports being in different somatic systems other than the nervous system, as in talking and thinking. These other systems afford a rich opportunity of dropping in and tuning into a different level, aspect, character, sound, and expression of the Self. Dancers feel connected deeply with no spoken words at all, as we move to the rhythms and pulsations of our own heartbeats together.

Silence really is a misnomer, though, because free dancing can get very loud at times. Sounds that erupt from the body, impulsively and physically, can happen anytime. These waves of energy move joyously around the room with velocity. Sounds may be low humming or high squealing, one never knows until that moment in which a sound wants full expression. Your body may need to beat the floor, or your feet might want to stomp the ground. The community too, may all drop into the same beat, clapping or stomping in rhythm, which can be a delightful sound to the ears.

Once we begin to listen through the body, we cannot help but become more empathic and intuitive to our surroundings. As these skills get easier, they benefit relationships in the long run. Honing the skills of tuning into people through body language (silent dancing) is one of the first strong and lasting benefits of free dance. For example, if someone approaches you with their arms crossed, you will recognize the language of the body as being pulled inward, their energetic space is closed. Now that you understand, you can be sensitive to this energy. You may move more cautiously than you once did, and slowly to enter their space with ease.

Personal safety is also an outcome of understanding body language and boundaries. Knowing when to exit a room or get out of the way of an angry or careless individuals will become more natural and immediate, because you will have gained a greater aptitude for reading body language in your surroundings, which will give you an edge on life. Learning to read body language is a great skill, but be careful not to apply judgement or projection to what you are seeing. I offer this reminder because, we in our programmed mind, like to apply stories to everything! My story of what you are doing will be based on my own perceptual grid of understanding or my own personal experiences from the past. For example, maybe you like to hold your head high. Therefore, in my story about you, I might think you are snobbish based on my aunt who also holds her head high, when in actuality; you are simply gazing at the clouds and enjoying yourself. You see, right there, out of my own life experiences I have applied a story onto you that absolutely has no validity, nor is it fair. So remember, when we apply judgement to someone's actions, we might short-circuit a possible connection with that person. Cultural conditioning causes us to judge others by the way they look, stand, talk, eat or dress. Refraining from superficial judgement, therefore, is a good habit to form, especially when we want our world to open up and receive us just as we are. I say this as a reminder because the person being judged just may hold the key to your next adventure, job, or relationship. Anything can unfold, and you will never know unless you stay open. Allow everyone to have unique expressions, ways, and beliefs because this is when life will move away from being stuck and stagnant to being more open and flowing.

Sometimes adults who have lived in dangerous situations in childhood seem to have a highly tuned ability to read, react, and respond to unspoken emotions. Survival may have depended on reading unspoken signs and reacting quickly.

In community dance, that skill becomes a conduit for joy and connection, instead of a conduit for fear. Free form dance transforms hyper-vigilance into heightened vitality. This is good news for everyone!

Dancing without talking opens up a new channel within you to be born. The channel to deeper listening, trusting intuition, communicating through your body, and following your flow allows you to access all the other ways you can communicate effectively.

Silence

Silent dances, bodies

talking,

Melting in rhythm

with many different

People at one time.

Feeling into the messages of love, compassion,

and Joy.

Words are not necessary for the

body tells all.

Pulsing, quickening, suspended, and surrendered

The language is new, different,

Ever defining.

Bumps in Bliss

While dancing in the midst of 50 or more people, at one time or another, you will get touched, bumped or even tripped. You see, when you are dancing and the energy is moving, the moment a bump happens, the energy stops. It is up to you how you respond. You have the choice to remain open and responsive with this energy or react to it out of old habits. If someone bumps into you while dancing, it can become part of your dance. You can take that energy and work with it, move it, and create pathways with that dancer. Or, that bump may just freeze right there in the moment, and your choice is to smirk and grumble, going into judgement, and blame the person, which inhibits all the fun. You can also move away from the bump, flowing inward if needed, dealing with it as you need to. It's your dance; your experience.

Of course, at times there may more than a bump. If so, take care of yourself by taking the appropriate action. Be brave. Nurture yourself however you need to take care of your feelings in the moment of unintended contact. The dancing community generally responds with kindness for you if you do get hurt, and you can connect with the facilitator or teacher if you need direct support. Also, find the courage to approach the person after the dance and share your experience. Who knows? The collision may blossom into a friendship and many more dances with that person.

Bumps and bruises happen in all kind of ways in our lives. We get our toes stepped on, and it can trigger feelings that we've hidden in our hearts about losing a job, or a cheating lover, or a death in our family. Anger flares! Someone did not see your presence, but it doesn't mean that you're invisible. Losses happen. We lose friends, lovers, we lose a job, a lover cheats on us, we get in a car accident, we lose any number of things from car keys to homes. All these bruises can merit a reaction. Sometimes we will grumble and moan. Wailing can be a tremendous release of pain. When a smaller bump or bruise results in a huge reaction, it may be because that bump touched a deeper, unexplored or hidden place of pain, so take care of yourself.

If you have unprocessed pain from your past, bring it to the dance floor; dance it! If this is not enough, make sure to get the support you need off the dance floor, through whatever means work for you. Some of us with pain stored in our bodies have found tremendous relief from regular massages, somatic therapy, or free writing in nature. It is essential to own and process your experiences.

As a freedom dancer, it is my hope that as dancing becomes part of your being and practice, going with flow will happen more easily. You will reduce your reactivity and initiate the actions you need to feel truly free from past wounding as well as the bumps and bruises that happen in the now.

Questions to ask Self:

• Do I feel too close to this person?

• Do I feel empty after a certain person leaves my dance?

• Do I want to lose myself in the mix of the dancing mayhem?

• What is it I prefer in closeness to some dancers over others?

Let Go & Trust

Generally, in the practice of most conscious dance venues, the music will get louder and the beat gets stronger, you might want to use earplugs if you are sensitive. Dancers may look like they have tranced out, or look wild to someone unfamiliar with the practice. As the music heightens advanced dancers let their bodies go. They go in all directions and at all speeds. Indeed, the fun intensifies to a fevered pitch, with full permission to be big, wild, and carefree!

Gabrielle Roth, the founder of 5 Rhythms, refers to this interim in her trademarked dance outline as Chaos, and it is truly is set up to be this way. The music is designed to get under the skin and shake the life out of us! By the life, I mean the energy that has been burdening, restricting, forcing or unfulfilling living and stored in the body. Other dance forms vary from the 5 Rhythms, but many are somewhat the same. The 5 Rhythms, according to Roth, are Flowing, Staccato, Chaos, Lyrical and Stillness. Before we settle down into bliss we must go fast and/or deep to experience that high energetic place where all constrictions falls away and the life force expands and takes over. The energy may even open up into an energy orgasm, an explosion of internal energy that can give you goose bumps or streak from your toes through the top of your head. The more chaotic dance you can muster, the greater potential of freedom you will experience.

While the music is more intense, practice the In/Out exercise mentioned earlier, being with Self, pulling inward; expanding outward. Make eye contact. Play with separation and joining as you dance. Be free! Notice the different feelings you experience as you go near others. One person may seem exciting, while another seems sultry. One may seem boring, when another feels familiar. Free movement creates a place where every emotion can be observed among dancers all over the dance floor. Look around the room at the swirling energies of all these people dancing. You will see hard and sharp moves; soft and subtle tones; flowing and consistent patterns; facial expressions offering love, anger, fear, confusion and celebration.

Dancing freely thrives on a beautiful accepting atmosphere where every emotion is permitted and invited to become part of the whole! Wow, what we all have wanted for so many years: free movement, instead of having to conform and behave!

Dance Sober, Everyone

Many of us have been moving freely on the dance floor for a long time inebriated. Two beers, courage to loosen up, and attempt to get on the dance floor, is our culture's present and most popular way for people to be at ease, feel sexy, join others and move the body. These alcohol-induced dances are not about feeling feelings or dropping into a heartfelt dance with another. It is the pump, the "look at me I am so great" dance, and "hey baby you wanna?" dance. There are no boundaries, respect, or safety in these kinds of dances, much less a sense of conscious awareness.

Authenticity dissolves in an alcohol or drug-induced haze, and that kind of dance, the opposite of community dance, reduces genuine feelings and awareness. The lack of inhibitions engendered by consuming alcohol and drugs has no place in free form dance, which focuses on finding feelings, not masking them.

We reach a place that is not about the beer buzz, but about the natural high experienced from feeling our feelings, expressing ourselves through movement, and communing with others in a loving way. We create safe places that lift spirits naturally and hopefully act to disparage the "meat market" mentality. Dancing freely is about the individual exploration and dance with Self, giving completion and connection without the need of a partner or any false, temporary changes in our state of being.

I understand that alcohol gives us courage and many of us have not yet experienced communing with others socially without a drink in one hand. The only place many of us have participated in this kind of social event, is probably Church.

In the subculture of ecstatic dance we have no drink in the hand, we are fully exposed in our bodies and ourselves to each other, this takes courage and desire. The wonderful thing is you have permission to do whatever you want. No one is going to expect you to play, act or dance when you do not feel like it. You can hide, if needed, staying curled up in a ball in the corner if this is your authentic expression.

This practice is fun and delightful especially when we experience the magic of true connection. Alcohol is simply a numbing device to keep us shut down and living a lie inside of ourselves. When we touch because we truly want to and are led from the heart we feel the essence of what free form dance truly is.

Avoid the Co-Dependent Dance

Self-expressive dance is about the individual dance that can only come from the individual, not the partner, or the need for a partner. Two halves may make a whole, but in free form, each person reaches inner wholeness, and the resulting connections come from a place of strength. Although you can have an excellent time dancing with a partner during this kind of exploration, it is not the focus.

We avoid the co-dependent dance. In co-dependent dancing we wait for someone else to make the move to the dance floor, seek validation or approval from our partner, hope people think we dance great, and unconsciously mirror moves without feeling, mostly.

How many of us fall in the shadow of another or seek approval? Do we do what others do because it is easier or just a plain habit that has gone unnoticed for quite some time? Sounds like a bad relationship, right? Exactly!

Remember all those times in the past when you got up the courage to dance on your own because that song moved you differently than it did your friend? Right there you mustered up the nerve to dance by yourself, partner or not. Free style dance as a practice is about original self-expression, not hiding behind someone else's moves.

Dancing fluidly and independently comes naturally when we remove our co-dependence on others. Many dances have steps and forms that have been handed down and refined for multiple generations, and those dances have beauty, meaning, and place. Free form dancing has no prescribed steps that must be followed in a certain order. Instead, you dance from connection, from feeling, and from the rhythms that vibrate within you with the mood and the music.

Dancing freely is wonderful fertile ground to gain more awareness of the relationship tendencies playing out your personal life. You can watch yourself and observe how you may tend to cross boundaries, how abrupt your energy is at times, your need for attention, and your sense of separation and hurt when someone leaves you for another dancer. All these poignant details in relationship play out right there on the dance floor. As you practice the teachings in this book and begin to understand the art of Self Witnessing, you also will begin to notice how you are showing up in relationships. Please understand I am not saying, "no partners!" Exploring the nature of your own moving body comes first, and connections may come when you've entered that centered, free-flowing place.

Know your **Body Systems**

System I - FAT
Heavy, round, slow, comforting, nourishing, warm, lethargic

System 2 - BONES
Thin, quick, dry, loose, careless, free-falling, swinging

System 3 - ORGANS
Round, slow, emotional, comforting, needy, tender, warm, closeness, deep

System 4 - NERVOUS
Busy, active, talkative, hyper, stressed, quickness of breath, abrupt, dry, hyper focused

System 5 - MUSCLES
Strong, defined, powerful, defended, armored, steady, grounded, fixed

System 6 - ENDOCRINE
Sexy, sensual, soft, playful, charismatic, exuberant, joyful, energetic, alive, spirited

System 7 - FLUIDS
Carefree, whimsical, light hearted, easy, go-with-the-flow, transitional, no obstacles

Bonnie Bainbridge Cohen, the founder of Body-Mind Centering, refers to seven systems in the body, and theorizes that each of us operate from one or more of these systems predominantly. The systems are: fat, organs, bones, fluids, muscle, nerves, and endocrine. She has found in her studies that we interact with our world and other people through a dominant system and do so out of formed, habitual patterns of human development. It is generally out of comfort and survival that we tend to drop into a major system and unconsciously stay there.

Understanding this phenomena and using it to our benefit can greatly increase our potential for a more satisfying life and positive relationships. Playing with this knowledge can feel like fascinating exploration. Ask yourself which category feels most comfortable to you. Generally, there is dominant and less dominant system in your body. Become aware of these body systems, and learn to encompass all of them in order to have a greater movement palette and different approaches to your everyday world.

Review the chart about Body Systems, then take a look at the people next to you, and become curious. Does that person live from their nervous system or their bones? Take a moment to study movements, body types, ways of speaking. They may be a combination of two, but once you begin getting more investigative you can discern how these systems show up, often quite dramatically.

A predominantly nervous system person will be super organized, thinking their problems through and constantly on the move, whereby an organ person will move slower, speak more quietly, and often be quite empathic to another's need.

Once you begin to discern the differences, you will be able to access a different system whenever needed in your own life. Instead of living constantly and unconsciously from one dominant system, you can choose where you want to focus your attention and how you want to encounter and embrace the world around you.

The beauty of acknowledging their existence grows as you begin to make conscious choices. I can very much get stuck in my nervous system, trying to think about what I am going to write, versus dropping into my fluid system and allowing the words to appear on the computer screen with ease and grace. The fluid system alone, though, may result in incomprehensible gibberish to others, so the systems work together to create a cohesive communication.

You see, each system has its strengths and is here to support us however necessary, but it is up to us to remember their gifts and know we can access these at any time. Play with them, explore them, and push your comfort zone.

Let's try a conscious choice. Be in your fat today, really sink into that place, especially if you are mostly a muscle person. Fat for a muscle person is a no-no! Go ahead, though. All you have to do is feel into the fatty aspects of you, the softer, more pliable you. Let go and get comfortable. Dance from that system, and compare how it feels to dance from the various systems. You see, you are all of these things at any given moment and you simply need to become aware of one to explore its nuances and its contribution to your personality.

These systems have so much information for our long term development. They make us more of a whole human when we have access and use them. Running on one system too long will deteriorate the body, and eventually it will malfunction. Take notice everyday, if possible, to allow your systems to be interchangeable. Have fun.

Dance and Feel your Words

When I was a young girl at age 27, I lived in Berea, Kentucky, a beautiful Appalachian town. I was an undergraduate student and a single mother. During this time I was moving through lots of growth. One teacher, in particular, I remember well. She was a beautiful and mature wise woman living in the foothills of Kentucky. Rocking in her rocking chair on her front porch, she taught all those who cared to listen.

One teaching in particular, she shared, stands out. What she referred to as Slave Words, the words that hold us hostage, waste precious energy and create the same damaging result over and over again. She identified these words as guilt, shame, doubt, would, could, ought to, worry, fear, old, and lastly, believe. Yes, even this one! These words are our greatest enemy because they hold us back from being in the here now and rob us of our precious creative life force and the ability to expand into unknown realms safely.

Folks, these words rob us of our truest Selves. They are no good! We have many positive replacement words to use whenever we decide to utilize their strength. If we can choose our words, why not choose words that strengthen us, instead of that which destroys. We can decide in any moment to replace the action, thought, or word with a higher resonance of what will support to lives we choose to manifest.

We only have so much precious time to be our most wonderful selves in the world, and when we are tied up in any of these actions we simply are not available. Sometimes we get habituated to using these words and actions of negative vibration instead of learning to reprogram our thinking mind to replace them with what I refer to as freedom words that can change our life for the better. When we dance, we dance without words, but when we live our everyday lives they run the show.

As a dancer when I feel I have "fallen off the wagon" in my practice, my old self-aggression tends to comes out. The enslaving words begin: "wow, look at you, two weeks and your lazy ass should have been on the mat!" or "Oh boy, my body hurts, why have I been so lack in my discipline?" or " you see... we told you, you were old and no good, this proves it, look at your flabby muscles, your lack of endurance..." It goes on and on if I allow it, or become numb and unconscious to it. Luckily, I have learned to become my own self witness and stop and notice what I am saying to myself.

Dr. Masaru Emoto claimed that human consciousness has an effect on the **molecular structure of water** and describes what happens to a water molecule when we regard it with disdain or aggression. The water molecule looks toxic under a microscope, disorganized and eerie. However, he shares, if we regard the molecule with love, compassion and deep regard, it forms an amazing snowflake or mandala shape in perfect harmony. Yes, these findings have been remarkable and they share such deep wisdom into our own ability to become a toxic water molecule or a beautiful snowflake.

Self-love creates the beauty within, and self-aggression creates the opposite! So on your mat, or in the woods with your favorite music, doing some stretching, and breathing, be kind to yourself and pay attention to your words. Are they slave or freedom? Note the negative vibrations sent from you to you and decide, in that moment, to change it! You can do this but it takes practice!

Behavioral-cognitive therapy teaches this concept. Notice in that moment what you are thinking and saying to yourself, and decide to change it to something positive and something you want instead. My thoughts of aggression about being lazy simply change in an instant to "I forgive myself and I am here now exercising. Thank you, Body!" Sometimes we need to do this 50 times a minute until it becomes easier. Our conditioning has programmed us toward the negative, certainly not the positive, so it is up to us to change the deep ingrained habits of self-aggression.

I agree, it is not easy to rid ourselves of this habit, but it can be done. It is a simple trick of cognitive re-patterning. Every time you catch yourself thinking about something you have no control over, or worrying, try to gain control and stop it! You do have permission to change your mind and you can change your thoughts.

You see, cognitive therapy simply replaces new thoughts with ones that aren't serving your best and highest good. Your thinking mind will travel into the old grooves, so you need to pull your mind into the direction that you want to travel and to keep at it. Practice makes perfect. I have personally been working on this for years! If your mind insists on going into the direction that does harm, take a moment, get on a dance floor and dance yourself free. It is up to you to take hold of the wheel of your life and direct it to where you want to be in that moment.

Worry has got to be one of the most powerful, toxic, ways in which to skip over our own life force and be wrought with an incessant, uncomfortable energy. Think about how you feel when you worry. I bet if you were to take notice of your body when worrying, your belly is constricted; your head aches; you're lethargic and your energy is sour. Worry creates real physical issues. Changing your diet or your physical regimen is an excellent idea to feel better, but if you are not changing the habits of your mind, you simply are wasting time and money. Yes money because more that likely you are working to rid yourself of the discomforts of your body by going to specialists while continuing to worry. Allowing worry to continue in your consciousness continues to create the physical pain.

Dance Church

Some freestyle dances are referred to as a Dance Church, a theme of a particular dancing community. A Dance Church forms when the same group dances together often, and the dancers know one another as they build a sense of the collective community. Dance Church also encompasses the essence of a spiritual gathering and can be highly transformative for all who participate. Participants learn to trust other dancers and feel a sense of belonging. No, this is not a requirement, but generally self-generated as a byproduct of a close knit dancing group. We all know that isolation, fear, grief, and anger come from the natural well of human feelings and at times need safe space for experiential expression. The energy of the Dance Church creates an atmosphere where dancers sense their neighbors' troubles and tune into them with loving supportive attention.

Instead of, or in addition to, actively and solely praying together with words to console one another, dancers care for each other by witnessing the movement of the person, hugging, or hearing the story associated to the distress at the end of the exercise. Some silent Dance Church groups have a talking circle at the end, so that dancers who want to process their emotions can connect verbally. You are held with attention and compassion by the group, hopefully.

Dance Church is a way to fully be yourself, being seen for the complete human you are. When you leave one of these gatherings you may feel your spirit uplifted quite the way you may feel after a regular church service. Actually, and in all honesty, you may feel better because your prayers have been danced, felt, expressed, heard and expanded into the universe from your direct, attentive moving heart.

A unified group of dancing hearts has immense power! Power to heal, to change, and shift reality as we know it. When we harmonize on the same frequency with the same intentions while joyfully sending energy out through our hearts, we are unstoppable! Through a Dance Church experience, led by a powerful facilitator we can cultivate and generate an energetic wave that if given the right attention can be sent out to change the outcome of a future event or the destruction of a powerful storm. Yes! We can do this. I have seen this happen. Humans are super heroes when we align ourselves with each other and with the same intentions for healing.

Outcomes of the Practice

Unique Dances

A nugget that makes freestyle community dancing fabulous and beautiful: No two dances are ever alike! We create the opportunity for the aliveness of people to meld together and create a different experience every time they come together! On the outside, a free from dance community may look like a simple group exercise. In essence, though, what occurs inside of each dancer and in the collective feels different every time. Here you have a familiar place and space but no idea of what may unfold in the mix. The mystery of how that particular dance will unfold for you, everyone else individually, and the collective as a whole creates a fertile and rich ground for deepening connections.

One can watch this developing closeness naturally occur by noticing the initial theme of any group as they begin. The group may exhibit one theme and end up somewhere entirely different. For example, the group may be fragmented, as when each person appears distracted and dealing with heady stuff as they appear separate from the now and each other. Fragmentation can be a common theme in the beginning of most dances as individuals drop from the concerns of their minds into their bodies and feelings. Once the dance begins, the music shifts and the energy builds, the group energy will do the same. The group may rise together in one unit or drop into pairs that create linked dances. As the music declines in tempo there may be larger groups that melt into a puppy pile. Each dance, every time, takes on its own creation and becomes uniquely insular in its expression.

Thankfully, a sense of community is generally the outcome or theme of most free style dance events. The music lifts people's spirits and frees minds from concerns! Dancers remember the now, other people, and things that matter most! Ultimately, love and connection emerge.

No one has said that the free form dance practices are a place to fall in Love, but I believe that after you dance a few of these dances, you may find yourself open to Love in a whole new way. In actuality, when individuals are allowed to be themselves, express their feelings, follow their flow, and trust their instincts, how can Love not be present?

Holding Space

Holding the container or space in the practice of community dance means listening attentively and actively to the group dynamics and to each other. It can also be how we approach one another when listening to our fellow dancers share their stories. Having someone listen and witness can heal us when we are sharing our deepest issues. Holding a space of love is a compassionate act which gives the sharer quality time to be seen and heard for what is real, without anyone interrupting them and trying to fix or change their reality.

Well-intentioned friends often want to share their knowledge and expertise in the realm of self-development to show off their healing attributes, however, the person sharing their story may need something completely different. In an effort to help, others may begin to tell us how to fix the problem, overriding the tender moments of our vulnerable sharing. Rainer Marie Rilke, the poet, wrote that sometimes we do not know the answers, and we need to live the questions.

When others rush to solve our problems, the resulting mishmash can become an obstacle to our own journey to inner truth. It seems when this situation happens the listener either has too much to do to express authentic concern for the problem, or they can't handle the negativity of the situation and have an urgency to make everything smooth and familiar for their own comfort.

Holding space is a learned skill, but not a difficult one. To truly hold space for another human being's pain means to feel open, quiet, non-reactive, and caring for what is being felt, allowing every emotion needed to rise to the surface. Certainly, the witness practice is super important here because if at any moment the process feels like a personal confrontation or attack, then the act of holding space has clearly ended. If you feel you cannot give time or an ear to someone feeling pain, or feel your defense mechanisms kick in, politely let them know your truth. You can choose whether you have time to listen and you can separate yourself if you need to. You also can choose to own what might be coming up for you by sharing with them verbally that their intense sharing is uncomfortable for you. It may be triggering your own unhealed wounding.

All of us have issues that arise that need space to be processed in some way, some people, however, process through avoidance, hard work, or silent reflection, rather than through words and expressive arts. All of us deserve the right to choose our own ways. When we do hold space for another, however, let's listen empathically and not jump to solutions and conclusions too quickly. Give the sharer some space.

A good teacher in the practice of freestyle knows how to hold each and every person within their attention span. The dancers know they are seen and held. When a teacher speaks to a movement pattern that a person is doing, this helps the dancer feel accepted and seen for their unique ability to dance themselves free and to feel their own energy. A good facilitator is like a magician. They follow, they know, they are one with the moving group. They know when to enhance the music and when to slow it down. Many who are leading and teaching this modality are well trained. However, since it is a community dance, many are still learning.

When space is held inappropriately, one can sense the difference. Sadly, some teachers of the free style concept have not yet mastered the art of holding a container. The outcome is a sense of frenetic fragmentation, disjointedness, and crazy energy, (and no good for the dancer needing to go deeper). You always have permission to leave a dance if the container does not feel held. This is the difference between the ecstatic raves and the community dances/dance church. A dance church phenomenon will never occur if the teacher is unable to hold the container. It will simply be a bunch of expression with no glue to interconnect the dancers. Feel free to listen to what you need; what you feel; and what you want. This is your dance, after all.

Holding the container of love is two-fold: it happens individually, you with another; and, it happens dynamically, with the whole group. It is a learned process and takes time to develop. Once we all begin to pay closer attention and become more responsive to energy, we will be able to understand this concept more fully. It takes time and practice. Hang in there.

> Behind your thoughts and feelings, my brother, stands a mighty commander, an unknown sage.
> He lives in your body; he is your body.
>
> - Friedrich Nietzsche

Embodiment

From our fingers to our toes; our head to tail, we feel; we know; we are embodied. Yes, we do all have a body, but many of us do not live here or experience it fully. We dissociate or ignore our bodies' basic needs for pleasure, movement, and joy. The majority of people tend to live in the mind more often with thoughts, worries, fears, and stress which all happily take over the sense of Self.

The mind and its afflictions dominate as an unconscious habit. One that many never question. While in the mind, the body functions on auto pilot. It walks, reaches, extends, runs, it even does aerobic activity without needing any attention from Self. Auto pilot is how most people operate since we create habits which run our lives and responses.

Our living rooms, work-out gyms, and even schools, are hotbeds for auto pilot responses, or what is referred to disembodied awareness. We can sit in front of a TV all evening and pay attention to the shows while never paying attention to the body, the breath, or sensations for that matter.

The gym is the epitome of disembodiment! That's right. The place that is supposed to be all about bodies, disconnects spirit from body in the worst ways. Here we can run five miles on a treadmill while watching TV or reading a magazine and never once take note of the breath or what the body is feeling.

Ugly habits start early! By teaching children to pay attention to everything except their innate urges, drives, likes and dislikes in schools, children learn to avoid their bodily responses or at least compartmentalize them. They have to raise a hand to go to the bathroom, eat when they are told, not fidget or express themselves. Free expression will get you in trouble! We become conditioned to stay in the mind without any regard to the mind/body connection. The real message here is obvious: Do not feel!

Disembodiment, being separate from Self, has become standard in our culture. Living in bodies that are shut off from feelings make us sheep. Numbness emphasizes following the given path, working for someone else and never questioning the churning tensions in our guts that tell us when it is time to move on. How many jobs have you had where it was OK to feel an emotion or even express it for that matter? Moreover, many feelings from the past hurt, and we are experts at shutting down out of a sense of survival and it seems supported to do so in our culture. It's simple to turn off and ignore that which is uncomfortable. Shutting down and moving on is a survival skill, but the inner cost is extreme.

One problem with being out of touch with our uncomfortable feelings is that pleasurable feelings also get shut down. I am amazed as a sensual conduit how many people have a difficult time tapping into their erotica because the feelings are too intense to contain and control in customary ways. Some people even avoid sensual pleasures. They hold their breath; tighten the belly; ward off the feelings of ecstasy because they are feeling feelings, period. Somehow to feel has become taboo, too scary, too challenging.

Even the pharmaceutical companies shut people down from their true feelings. Drug inhibitors work by inhibiting your truest response to a stimuli. Yes, these medications serve a purpose for those who are truly in pain, but administering them to avoid feelings, at all costs, becomes a problem. Believe it or not, the natural ebb and flow of emotions in life belongs as an essential element in being human. The days when you or I feel something other than happiness can transform into true opportunity to dive in deep and meet it. When we do listen to the feeling we get to get curious. Is it vulnerability? Anger? Grief? What does it need from us to overcome its debilitating essence? By listening to our feelings and giving them their due, we become stronger and find our strength. Unfortunately, not many of us have the luxury to go deep into our feelings on a daily basis, so we have medication to support us. It helps us get up, pretend all is well, and march on to be productive citizens. When it numbs us from tuning into each other and our innate sense is when it becomes a problem. I ask some people how they feel and they answer, "I don't know." Feelings are human, once we learn to regard them with sincere attention and allow them to lead us to our inner truth, then we can begin to really heal.

Have you watched someone say one thing while all the signals of the body show the complete opposite? For example, a friend tells you he is feeling fine, but rubs his brow and has an expression of stress at the same time. You know what I am talking about, right? His actions clearly indicate his stress level, but his words say, "I am fine." Obviously, there is a disconnection between his mind and what he is feeling in his body. Others notice it, but he doesn't. When your friend is aware, and can admit he is stressed in his body, giving authenticity to the truth of his real feelings, then he is acting from a place of embodiment.

These feelings that live inside of us are the catalysts for our personal and transpersonal success. Therefore, finding ways to become embodied and practice listening to what your body has to say is a matter of survival not just a choice, as a human being!

So why care if we are embodied? From the standpoint of health and well-being, it is the precursor. Wellness derives from knowing what the body wants; when it wants it; how it wants to move; and what it is feeling in any given moment. We have the choice to stop and feel the body with the presence of our attention in any moment to practice the art of embodiment.

I invite you to try it right now. Close your eyes. Become aware of your surroundings. Listen to the sounds in your environment. Become aware of your breath, and notice what you are feeling, whether it is sadness, discontent, anger, or something else. Feel the feeling and come up a with a verbal description or metaphor. Maybe your anger feels like a ball of sticky prickles, or a flame; maybe your sadness feels like a well, or a congealed mass of pudding. Notice and feel whatever is going on inside of you right now. Do not judge it or create a story about why you feel what you feel, because that activity belongs to the mind. Instead, simply feel. Now, you are aware of You! Being attentive to you in this moment is the first step to becoming embodied. Recognizing and paying attention to what you really feel provides the key to embodiment. Once we begin to feel the emotions underlying our every move in relationship with other, while also being aware of the all-knowing Self, we are more congruent and balanced in our mind/body. Practicing free form movement then is an absolute positive way to become more embodied, as you ease from dominance by the mind, into the fullness of Self and in the feeling body.

Yoga is another wonderful way to become more embodied, since in a yoga class, the teacher is going to have you torque into an Asana or posture in order for you to feel something. Yoga works to awaken the body, bringing the mind/body attention to the Self to feel into the deepest parts of the you, and thus assisting embodiment to take place.

The benefits of being an embodied human are fabulous. We experience an overall sense of well-being. We also gain an early detection of illness, intuitively knowing if something is awry in our environment. We also generally experience a better sex life. Now, that's good news for everyone, right?

Mindfulness

Mindfulness acquired through free dance is the ability to pay attention to the moment and experience everything in that moment. When we are mindful, we are completely aware of what we are doing and experiencing. Mindfulness assists us in being completely awake. Let's look at the word, Mind-Full-Ness! When we bring attention to what is happening now, there is a better chance that life will be what we need it to be.

Mindfulness is primarily a meditation term, as in Buddhist meditation practice. It is also referred to as the "empty mind." When the mind empties of thoughts about the future, worries of the past, and other people, then there is room to be open to the moment and everything occurring within it. The empty mind is generally honed while sitting in one place in meditation. However, becoming an empty mind on the dance floor is much more fun and sometimes easier. Most often when sitting still, the mind tends to ramble. On the dance floor, however, you can move with your thoughts, being one with them and giving them expression and permission to move. Your mind empties as your body explores and expresses your feelings, and you live fully immersed in that present moment, practicing mindfulness.

The distracted mind dawdles, expending energy on thoughts such as worry, fear, inhibitions, work duties, and self-absorption. Unanswered, unsolvable thoughts distract us from the present moment and tend to get us stuck, holding us hostage! How much really gets accomplished when we think about tomorrow or worry about some issue from the past instead of being present right now?

As the dance happens, and mindfulness is being practiced, one can literally witness Self being in the flow or Self being stuck. Stuck in the dance may look like standing around watching others, unconscious of what is happening in your own body, and interested in everyone else, not yourself. Being in the flow appears vibrant and active because the energy literally moves you and moves through you. You awaken to the energy right there and move with it and into it. As we become more mindful, life seems to flow more easily. Staying in the flow gets our life moving and we follow what is in front of us, trusting that the way will unfold easily. A stuck life is stagnant. Too much thinking and nervous energy being wasted on nothing that leads no where. Mindfulness is an art and one must practice it in order to understand it. The dance floor is a wonderful laboratory for Self study. Staying open and aware of ourselves in every moment will gift us with insight we never knew we had.

> Compassion is not sentiment but is making justice and doing works of mercy. Compassion is not a moral commandment but a flow and overflow of the fullest human and divine energies. -Mathew Fox

Compassion

Attaining true compassion means working from a strong heart. We hold the moment, ourselves, and others in the light with grace, embodying the image of strength in the face of suffering. We have the strength of a willow tree, the strength of a river, able to bend and flow with the changing winds around us without breaking ourselves.

Many dictionaries define compassion as what sounds like sympathy or empathy. Feeling sorry for another as in sympathy, or empathy, feeling one's feelings. Compassion arising out of the free form movement practice is learning to accept others where they are without judgement or trying to fix them. Being loving, with a compassionate and open heart, does not mean being passive. Compassion emerges from strength, not from weakness! When we have true compassion, we do not turn away from suffering, but acknowledge and bear witness, holding others in the light of caring. The Dali Lama says that when we remove feeling and simply come to others with an open heart of understanding, we offer the art of compassion.

Compassion gleams in the act of allowing others to have their experiences while simply holding the space in your heart for them. We may be inspired, from our compassion, to act strongly to change a wrong, but in the moment of compassionate listening and witnessing, we simply observe and absorb with careful attention.

To practice compassion is to know and acknowledge suffering. Regarding someone from a position of love with an open and kind heart is to allow the person to be where and who they are, without interference or judgment. We refrain from needing to fix or do anything as a response out of our own wounding when we truly practice compassion. When I want to fix you out of my own discomfort, who am I truly serving?

The essence of compassion is sending Love to those who suffer, not angst in needing to fix.

In my practice as a Dakini (a sacred sexual healer) and a psychotherapist, I have worked with many people who appear to be suffering. Compassion allows an insight into the true beauty of the inner darkness and depths of others and of the Self. I have literally laid my hands on people who have killed people. Yes, men from the military. I had to allow them and love them to be who they were to feel their own experiences, to trust and stay open. I have also put my hands on a so-called "white supremacist" a time or two, getting under the wounding and seeing the Self underneath all of the hateful tattoos. His skin expressed deep hatred to humanity, but I, as a compassionate being, worked to see the basic goodness beneath.

I can have this compassion for their suffering because I, too, suffer and know what it is. Although, I may not have shared the same experiences as them. The fact is, however, when we strip away all of our identities, belief systems, political views - we are all the same.

Judgement often arises out of wanting a person to be like me, or thinking something is wrong with them, instead of simply holding space for their pain. Judgement also comes from the place of needing to fix. Now, nothing is inherently wrong with fixing or repairing, but compassion begins with simple recognition of human beings, ourselves and others, in distress. Simply being there, without judging or analyzing, to listen and accept, often allows others the space needed to find their own answers and create pathways to personal growth.

Many years ago, I worked as a therapist with sexually abused traumatized children, I did not take label or judge as good or bad. Instead, I opened my heart in compassion for all the trauma the children had endured and experienced in their brief lives. Allowing a child, with deep suffering, to be accepted through my understanding of their pain, opened the door to a shift in their self-perception and progress.

Children and adults find ways through terrible pain when they experience true compassion and unconditional acceptance from another. This compassion encourages deepened inward reflection, and acknowledges the anguish that may have been hidden. Being loved for exactly who we are will shift any person's consciousness right there! Nothing else is needed for the healing to begin.

Take a moment now to imagine being accepted and loved for all that you are right now, your bad habits, your suffering, your pain, your challenges, your strengths, all of it! You! Right now being loved!

Compassion for Self can feel like a dance of the heart. Allowing yourself to be and feel all that you are, without trying to fix or change it, can be the beginning of your own inner dance to a fuller and more fulfilling life. When we sense that someone judges us, and sees us as imperfect, we hide parts of true nature to please them. When we hide who we really are and what we truly feel in hopes of achieving acceptance or inclusion, we soon find that projecting a persona takes time away from truly nurturing the inner wisdom of the Self.

In my personal quest to evolve, I have found it easier to be compassionate to others before practicing compassion to myself! It seems, from my own experience, and those I have counseled, that we constantly negate our habits and our survival mechanisms. We wish they would go away or disappear and we make them wrong because we think they are not serving our best selves or the Self we want to be. Does this sound familiar? If so, please hold compassion for you; embrace you; send love to parts of you that sabotage or retreat in places of fear and uncertainty. Yes, even you deserve compassion from yourself to yourself. Maybe the best way to become familiar with the practice of compassion is to begin with your own wounding, your own mishaps in life. Accept it as is, with love.

Expansion

We live in a contracted society. The idea of expanding fully into our bodies and our fullest expression receives very little support in most segments of our lives. We often get encouraged to shrink ourselves to fit into tiny emotional spaces, thinking small, holding back, swallowing our feelings and constricting our flow. Free movement and dance gives us space, time and permission to feel these feelings and to be as big as we want to be, so we can then expand into our larger world and feel the joy we are intended to feel.

Expansion means truly taking up space outwardly. Many people exist throughout the day with life held tight and pent up without even realizing it. This tendency seems quite bizarre if we really look at this with a closer eye. Here we live in the Universe, so big, expansive, accepting, and loving, and yet we have become quite adept to pulling inward and suffocating our life force to the degree that heart attacks, dis-eases, and depression grow rampant.

Let's look at the word "depression" for a moment. Depression is a feeling of heaviness, despair, giving up, feeling isolated. Think about these. Feel them!   Now think of expansion into joy, lightheartedness, ease, and fullness. Feels different, right? Yes, not all of us feel safe with the feeling of expansion, especially if we are habituated to holding ourselves back. It can be quite scary to reach outward.

One particular child client of mine, I remember well, was a young boy who was contracted and intimated by life. I asked him to outstretch his arms and reach upward until he started to feel unsafe and then stop. His arms went out half way, a bended elbow stretch, not a long reaching movement at all. He was unfamiliar with the process of expanding in his body, much less his Self. As we continued our work together he gained courage. He began to extend his arms further each time, becoming more comfortable in his skin and developing more social skills at the same time. How comfortable are you with reaching outward? Try it now. How far can you extend in the space around you and trust you are safe?

When you first awaken, do a little stretching before you get out of bed. Make movement part of your everyday life, awakening with a dance to the doorway as you step outside to breathe a moment of fresh, pure air. You can dance and expand gently as you make breakfast, or make dressing into a dance. Move, move, move those arms and legs! Dance alone in your bedroom, your kitchen, your living room. Dance when no one's watching, to the rhythms of your own heartbeat and the music in your heart. Allow expansion to happen consciously. You choose this path. As you become more familiar with the art of dancing freely and expanding, you may still enter a group practice feeling constricted before you begin. Drop deeply into that constricted place first, give it an expression, a sound, a tone. Feel it, be it, become it and watch how your body naturally finds its way through it to a more expansive feeling, sending energy outwardly.

You live in your body; you are your body; the more comfortably your body moves, the more joyfully you will live in this world. When we start stretching our legs, moving feet, ankles, tightening, and loosening each muscle group, our bodies and minds begin to flow in harmony. Beginning in an authentic place and being with whatever you feel, moving, stretching, and expanding shifts the mind. Truly listening to your own impulses and practicing this everyday will most certainly begin to change your life over all. Listening to your body and giving it permission to move how it wants to opens a doorway to discovering parts of Self. Expressive movement builds new pathways to explore life differently. Over time, you will be reaching out for those things that satisfy you more easily and with more confidence than ever before just by getting comfortable moving your body in new, expansive ways.

> Our deepest fear is not that we are inadequate.
> Our deepest fear is that we are powerful beyond measure.
> It is our light, not our darkness that most frightens us.
> We ask ourselves: Who am I to be brilliant, gorgeous,
> talented, fabulous?
> Actually, who are you not to be?
> You are a child of God.
> Your playing small does not serve the world.
>
> --Marianne Williamson

Being Seen

Dancing brings up feelings. The feelings of emptiness, being unloved, forgotten, overlooked, and abandoned. We can dance through these experiences and dance into the release of these feelings. Questions may emerge that you have kept you low for a long time, such as "why I am not loved like my brother or sister appear to be loved?" "Where are my parents emotionally and why can't they connect with me deeply?" Most of our parents did not wake up to their magnificence and were unable to see ours. They may have been emotionally shut down or constricted. When people are constricted themselves out of fear or habit, it is difficult to be available to others.

Why do you think abandonment is such a huge word in our culture? Since our best selves were left without reflection to us, a part of us may feel like it's missing. People become codependent because they have a void of Self, that place where the essential human being longs to meet itself. If someone does not know themselves, how can they truly see another? If we do not know who we are it may be because we did not get an accurate reflection of ourselves in childhood. Even if we had supportive parents, we may not realize or accept who we truly are because the only time we received recognition was when we did something wrong. The only time we felt seen may have been when we were called out by angry elders.

When you dance, it doesn't matter if you are like anyone else, because essentially you're not! When you dance, you experience your entire body as a flowing life force and will begin to see yourself and others through a more vibrant, true lens. Free form dance finds you and sets the Self free. Dancing freely can end feelings of abandonment, because when you dance, you become intimately and fully connected with a force of nature and spirit greater than yourself. You find intimate connections with other dancers who reflect your magnificence back to you. Whatever your spiritual path, when you dance, you will feel your own feelings more fully and completely, with an opportunity and path for unleashing them.

Seeing Others

In community dance, we are seen by many loving individuals in the group dance, people who are at the same time waking up to their own glorious and magnificent Selves and able to reflect ours! Wow! What great news!

Being seen feels good. However, it can be scary at times, since it brings up all those things we really do not want to know about who we are. This power of authentic movement allows us to find our flaws, feelings, and fantasies without judging. We get to choose how we want to move on the dance floor which carries over in life, as well. In dance, as in life, we can move forward or backward, sideways or in circles, and we can stand still. We get to see the other parts of the Self with compassion and acceptance.

As we learn to be seen, we also learn to see others for their beauty, essence and divine nature. We become more comfortable with the Self, so we extend further to create comfort for another by seeing them. Part of learning to expand both physically and energetically is learning how to extend and witness someone besides the Self. When we speak of seeing, we do not mean an action taken solely with the eyes, but an experiential and in-depth observation through all the senses of all the elements of ourselves and others. Many Gurus sit in front of their students, and completely and without flinching, look at them. The result is amazing. It is as if this human with unconditional love and inner Self love can reflect this energy back to us. This revered reflection of love from another helps us truly remember who we are.

Our society is self absorbed! It seems that many people spend more time looking at phones and computers more than they spend gazing into another's eyes. Children, friends and family crave attention. Quality of attention requires true presence. When quality attention disappears, I can look at you all day, but if my mind is distracted, I am not being truly present with you or seeing you. When we take the blinders off created by our own problems and issues we can clearly see others with love and send this outward to affect the world ten-fold.

We can choose, on the dance floor, to dance wide open, and in making that choice, we show all that we feel and all that we are. We can choose to close in ourselves like dark stars. We can choose to cast rays of light across the room. Once we know ourselves, we can begin to know others, and see others in a deepened and deepening way.

The Shine of the Inner Crystal

Dancing freely radiates vitality! I like to refer to this shine as the Inner Crystal. Over time, in the practice of free dancing, you will discover deeper aspects of your most beautiful self. The place that shines emanates from your innate essence of beauty, wisdom, and character. Dancing freely moves our bodies! We feel good. We shine. We have a healthy glow. We release old stuck energy and bring in fresh, new energy. We become more open, more receptive, more fluid, and tend to like life a lot more!

Making the conscious choice to peel away the layers, dig out what matters most, and clear the debris of old mistakes, abuse, and trauma, this will free the Inner Crystal- that aspect of yourself that is brilliant, diamond, stunning -- the truest part of your human nature and individuality.

Gemstones develop by the earth bearing down on them over long periods of time. To purvey a gemstone is hard work and one must dig deep. The same with the Inner Crystal. Both discoveries require concentration and focus.

As a rock, through years of hardship, develops an amazing gemstone beneath layers of earth and stone, so too do we develop an Inner Crystal through trials and tribulations. It is up to each of us to decide if we want to search for this crystal that lives deep within, and the methodology in which to find it.

Our early childhood challenges give us, as adults, reasons to become introspective, contemplative and to reach for answers beyond our conscious minds - if we choose to. Early childhood challenges can be opportunities for us to expand and grow into strong, and vital humans. Very few of us have perfect childhoods and therefore, all of us, have inner-work to do as adults. It is when we ignore and shut down these opportunities that life becomes dull and lifeless. We must decide to search within to release our own, authentic, genuine selves if we are to ever reach a state of pure euphoria in life or the dance floor.

I am offering to you the wisdom of conscious dance to seek and explore the hidden aspects of your being to hopefully render free the gemstone that lives deep within you. Once you find this place, no one can ever diminish it. It shines brightly and strongly. People feel your Inner Crystal when you walk into a room. You emanate love from your heart in a confident, self assured manner. No longer is baggage, blockages, or old yuck diminishing your shine. Finally, the path was laid and you had the courage to dance upon it, shedding old skin, renewing a deep sense of purpose in your life.

The Inner Crystal is always there. It is whether we want to dig deep, move through the chaos, merge with the flow, dive into the depths of our shadows and claim it for ourselves.

I know you have the inner strength for this, otherwise you would not be reading this book. Yes. You. You have this Inner Crystal that is beaming deep inside you. Allow it, find space to express it, it is fun, maybe even scary, but, so what, do it anyhow for your self development and everyone else around you. When you begin to shine, other people see this, they wonder how you found it. Be the leader. I surmise that everyone truly wants to shine their own Inner Crystal that is somewhere down deep. It may be up to you to show the others the way.

The Advanced Practice

Trance State

In the free style conscious dance practice, there comes a time when the mind empties into the glorious moment at hand, and the Self becomes entranced by the moment. The music absorbs all of you, and there is this deepening and quickening of nothingness that engulfs your Spirit. You become one with each drumbeat, the pluck of the strings, the whistle of the flute. Deeply you have dropped into the inner world, the greatest surrender, allowing all energy to come forth as you rest into the center of awareness. Many tribal cultures would attain this trance state in ceremony. The Whirling Dervish is a good example of this. They spin in circles going deeper and deeper in the moment, forgetting they live in a human body and become part of the unified field of others.

The Trance begins when we let go of anything that feels stuck, uncomfortable, and uneasy. We then begin to merge into oneness and joy; dancing hard, moving truth, aligning with source, and tuning into a higher vibration of consciousness.

The Trance State is a higher dimension than we spend time in everyday in our regular lives. It is a sense of soaring above the clouds, a freedom that we are spirit and spirit alone with expanded wings of the greatest eagle. There are no ties, obligations or pain. Acquiring this state of mind means we have done the work to release the stuff that unconsciously exist in our personal universes and have brought them to surface for inspection and release.

The onion, the Disney character Shrek speaks of, applies to us all. Utopia is not accessible when we have baggage. We must peel away the layers of old, useless, heavy, toxic energy; whether it is energetic, emotional, or the food we ingest, to break free to feeling the trance in life we are so deserving to feel.

It is up to us every single day to take notice of what is holding us down and do something about it, whether is dancing freely, or speaking with a therapist!

The Energy Orgasm

O! The Energy Orgasm has
become my favorite experience as
I grow deeper into myself and my
dance. Yes, the big O! I
differentiate the Energy Orgasm
from the physical orgasm. It is still an orgasm,
and, yes, all orgasms are energy, but what I am
getting at with the Energy Orgasm is the channel
it takes to reach this state of feeling. Physical
orgasm emerges with physical contact. Energy
Orgasms extend from energy being absorbed
and released.

In the practice of dancing our own dance we can
experience an Energy Orgasm. It is when all of
our bodies are aligned and feel completely
surrendered, safe, and supported in an
energetically rich and beautiful way. All
thoughts, held places, fears or constructs,
dissolve, and we feel the body shudder, as we
actually feel the kundalini (our life force) rise
through the body and out through the top of the
head. When we have graduated into a grounded,
assured place on the dance floor we can drop into
the body and out of the mind deeply to let go
and become but a pebble in the stream, gliding
and free floating to any place, to anyone,
through any movement at any time. This
miraculous dance; moving into and out of,
merging and swirling, breaking loose from and

dipping into, and all of the sudden, before you know it, there is a vortex, a whirlpool of sorts, where the Self has disappeared and has merged with the energy of life. A moment of divine delight surges into the Energy Orgasm!

When we, as physical beings, forget our physicality and inhibitions, and completely let go, then we have room for cosmic energy to fill us completely, with love lifting our Souls to the heavens. In these moments, we are reminded of our immense power as true spiritual beings. We can embrace, explore, and expand our power.

In my opinion, the Orgasm deserves to be revered and placed on the wake of every altar out there.

When have you had your best orgasms? Most likely with people you felt very safe with, your level of anxiety was very low, you felt sexy, open, your breath was moving, there was a deep connection with a person in the moment or in a lifelong way.

All dancers can feel the freedom of the Energy Orgasm, and it is a safe, sacred way to feel pleasure. For dancers who are single or working through relationship issues and refraining from direct contact with another, the dance floor can become a wonderful place to return home to your sexy self and become reacquainted with those fabulous natural sensations that your body knows so well.

You know that wonderful feeling after an incredible love-making experience? You know, the glow, the relaxation, of perfect health you feel after letting go completely? In free form dance, we get to experience this feeling too! Wow, what fun, indeed!

Surrendering into a place of the unknown, allowing it to be without control of any kind is when we experience the best orgasm. Staying true to our practice, going deeper with our emotional body, and giving ourselves permission to expand and let go, we can discover this sensational bliss. Getting on a dance floor for free form movement is the first step.

The Tantric Dance

I will not cover my breasts due to your discomfort.
I stand strong as a woman empowered in Self, Sexuality,
Sensuality, and SASS!
I am fullness of life itself.
The freedom in which my breasts dance carelessly but willfully
fills my essence of the truth of my femininity!
She Dances!
She plays!
She excites wholeheartedly.
That which I am is Love Manifest!
In deep strength
I surrender to the bliss of me!
I invite your masculine to join me in the connection that is us
and us alone!
Feeling of your magnitude engulfs me,
Blossoming and unfolding into the truest power of all that is.
Your masculine fills me
To lengths I have yet to know.
We discover eternity.
Magic enlightens my present mind-so completely.
I am filled with the universal charge of the every galaxy that
lays before us.

Tantric Dance

The Tantric Dance melts into the moment when we align with another human being. The moment matters, paramount and without pretension, in a total absence of stories of what the experience might become. You and your partner connect completely in that moment with all your senses.

Tantra, an ancient art, understands the power of the energetic exchange because when two meet on the plain of complete nothingness and immaculate sensation, we realize clearly we are not separate. The only thing that matters in the moment is the delicious breath, heartbeat, smell, touch of the person who's touching you, and the radiant energy of the place where the breathing comes into synchronicity. Each movement radiates from one to the other, creating an invisible but complete figure eight of energy. This energy takes the form of the symbol for infinity, and glides around you and through you. Synchronized energy and intimate knowingness dominate this dance. Neither one of you lead with the mind or the body. Instead, you both allow the energy between you to move your body and create the experience. You flow into the unknown and enjoy where it leads, trusting in the fact that this individual is so connected with you through the mystery of unconditional love, that no matter what you do in the next moment, your partner will be there for you. You join, always in forward movement into the next co-creative action.

The beauty of getting familiar with dancing freely, and watching it unfold into a tantric dance, is that we begin to see how we get in our own way in ordinary situations. Dancing with others can be mechanical and boring, with a complete absence of connection, or it can be a tantric dance, exciting and mysterious.

Life away from the dance can also feel mechanical because the constructs are so set. We want to force our life in a certain direction and will try very hard at times to make it work. How many times will we experience this kind of frustration until we realize that there is a natural flow to things and all we have to do is surrender and accept?

When we think we have to be something other than what we feel most deeply, our lives then become shallow puddles. We dam the flow of the eternal river of love and compassion that is our birthright. When we decide we want a different experience, we need to trust and learn to allow this river to flow. This ability soon blossoms into a natural state as we float home to our amazing selves and our greatest potential.

When we live in flow with mystery and wonder, we end up meeting fabulous people, experiencing amazing things and achieving our hopes and dreams.

Practicing the art of allowing and trusting life to happen, I personally met the Guru Dr. Wayne Dyer (RIP) when I lived on Maui. He was one of my personal clients in my healing practice. I could have never made this happen on my own, forcing it to happen, but being open and flexible with my time and living in the moment, resulted in an amazing connection. Yes, even this amazing man needed healing.

One of his teachings, I remember as his student (not his healer), is that a baby knows how to grow in the womb, no one tells it how! It just does. A plant also knows how to grow without any instruction. It needs water and sunlight, just as we do, but it grows by itself, trusting it will have space to expand and clean air to breathe. The Sun does not need to know how to shine. The moon, and a woman's moon cycle, needs no instruction to wax and wane. These are all natural occurrences that create life in a harmonious, healthy fashion. We, however, have been taught that we have to make life go a certain way and need struggle to survive, that we must control our environment if we are to be successful, safe, and loved in society. Illusions of control and safety are two constructs that can keep us downtrodden, disconnected from our personal power and unable to feel the pulse of ourselves in life and on the dance floor.

Authenticity grows from deep within, and as this true Self strengthens, our essence shines. When the Inner Crystal is aglow and all constructs and resistances have fallen away and surrendered, deep resonance of bliss emerges. We float home in the moment, unhampered by gravity. We exist in our truest selves joining with others lost in time.

Self Care is Word

Every one of us needs down time, which in turn is really deep time - time to explore our deepest selves and hear our own directives for that day. While being with Self in our solo practice, we practice many of the same techniques as we do in free form dance community circles, but we are the only one we are paying attention to.

Find nature, the ocean, a yoga mat, a clean room. Whatever creates a sense of serenity for you and drop into your own time! Play music and move. Dance naked, or in comfortable clothes. If you want, simply rest and listen to the music you love. Sing along, hum, holler, pound the floor, roll. Give yourself permission to be completely free.

Remember, it is a choice to take valuable deep time out of this crazy linear chaos. It is up to us to carve this hour out and when I say carve it out, I really mean it! I have personally found that this practice is amazing on resetting my attitude toward life.

Be careful, though, because when solo, what do we tend to do most? You got it. We often fuss about all the things we are not doing right or what we need to do tomorrow, should have done yesterday or what we are going to do next year! So bring attention to your thinking mind and listen intently! Thoughts stray into the next hour, to next week, next year, that person, that action. Whoa. Stop. Become aware. Breathe. Right now, stop all the enslaving words rolling around in your head and take stock of what your five senses tell you. What do you see, hear, smell, taste, feel? Bring yourself away from thoughts into this present moment. This tree, this yoga mat, this song. Exactly where you are now.

Objective Self Love means we discern how we are battering or loving self in each moment as we spend time in our own personal practice whether it is yoga, meditation or dance. At times, we can be our own worst enemies, or our dearest friends. We do get to choose how we treat ourselves.

Often the reason we tend to roam in our thoughts of the what we need to do is because we tend to fear the unknown. We think we need to figure it all out so we do not have to allow that unknown to occur. The truth is the unknown is where real information lives. Imagine for a moment that life is a big blank screen and that screen of nothingness means that you can create anything, at any time, to manifest your future! Good or bad. You are the orchestrator and the director of what life becomes! Yes, goals matter, and they help us manifest our dreams. Nonetheless, if we continue to lay our lives out six months in advance with our schedules full, then something as winning a fabulous trip or meeting that amazing person will not happen because there is no room for something spontaneous and new to enter. Your ego has taken control and figured it out for you and it usually is in a very limited fashion. Therefore, I support you to get out of your own way, free your schedule, get comfortable by yourself and with not knowing the future and you will, by surprise, unleash your potential you never knew you had.

Self Care is an imperative practice for all of us. If it isn't dancing in the woods, maybe it is taking a long hot bath. The real ingredient that makes it rich is the attitude and the attention you bring to the experience.

<u>Totality</u>

This book is finally ready for flight after the first words being written five years ago. Being a new author is very scary. All these words imparted from my Soul to yours. Now the important part begins, trusting that something in these pages has brought you closer to your true calling - not just how to freely dance. What matters to me as a teacher is providing the groundwork for you to literally dance toward your innermost freedoms, laying the path, the floor, the walkway, whatever it is to discover the deepest Self longing to become.

I happened to be in St. Louis during the Eclipse of 2017, able to spend a day where people from many walks of life focused fully on the "now" moment. I felt into the ethers of connection to all those souls who held the same joy, the same wonder, the same enlightened amazement during this event. When the Eclipse moved from Totality to the first light, I imagined it pouring into every heart, all over America!

This light -- brilliant, illuminating, dynamic and wonderful -- returned in such awe to all of us who were listening and needing to feel a deep source of connection. We danced together in rhythm, in harmony, and in peace as we collectively, knowingly or not, became instruments of the orchestra of this life, this Oneness that we all share in every moment.

The day before the Eclipse I swam in the amazing spring-fed lake on The Magic Land in Grubville, MO. The sky was beautiful and the clouds made the word ME. My friend and I laughed and in the next moment, I realized that ME is also WE, from a different angle.

In our conditioning, we are made to believe we are singular, solo, separate from each other, so our first inclination to see the clouds form letters M and E is to think ME! Yes, we are a ME, but all our ME's become a fabulous WE at anytime, anywhere! We can align with the angle or perspective we choose at any given moment.

Another teaching at this auspicious time in St. Louis comes from landing right smack in the middle of the city. Difficult? You could say that. A city is a huge challenge for me. I like quiet, meditative, tantric places of yummy vibration reflected back to me. I love the earth, the sky and nature. Wild beauty resonates high with my inner being. The city can be a struggle.

This morning while practicing self-care and dancing in the park, I was surrounded by the noise of traffic and the buzz of the city. It occurred to me that no matter where I find myself, my inner peace is constant. In the midst of chaos, noise, and people, inner peace never leaves me...I leave it! Once the message dropped into my consciousness, I listened, I practiced, and I felt so much better.

I'll share one more teaching from this great weekend before I depart. I was gifted with knowledge of how often I say, "I have work to do!" And feel the response as heavy and downtrodden. Yes, as a self-employed entrepreneur I have lots of work to do, always! Miraculously, in the next moment my guides whispered in my ear, "You have Love to share!" YES! I DO! and SO DO YOU!

When we are in our highest alignment with our Soul's calling, our work is the love we have in our hearts. Whether it is chanting, singing, painting, solving puzzles, cleaning houses, whatever it is that you gravitate towards as your heart's desire, there is no work to do... only love to share.

During my time this weekend I met new people, celebrating, too. My first impressions were that they were not much like me, and I wasn't sure I wanted to engage. I left the building and as I walked away, I remembered my own teaching from this book. I need to stay open and love these new people because they may hold a key for me.

As fate would have it, water and hearing aids do not mix, when devices get damp, they do not work. Ugh! So the night before the eclipse and the morning of that magic, I was without my devices. After the wonder and the amazement of the sun returning, I came back to the reality that my devices were plugged up. My new friend, one of the ones I decided to love instead of judge, offered to clean them.

These devices connect me to all things heard in my life. I took a deep breath and trusted that he knew what he was doing. Oh My Lord! He gave them to me and I could hear better than I have in a very, very long time. What a blessing and a key. My decision to be open and not react from judgement resulted in a new connection and a splendid gift.

Blessings to you my friends and may these words in this book continue to teach and remind each of you an easier way to dance yourself free and live the best life!

May the dance floor, wherever you find it, always help you connect with yourself, your true nature and the essence of all you are.

A HO!

About the Author

Leianna Love, a free spirit and free thinker, shares her love of life through dance and the human connection. As a solo artist and pioneer she earned a bachelor's degree in physical education and a master's degree in dance movement therapy and somatic psychology.

Leianna has been licensed as a clinical therapist in her past. In travels to Thailand, Maui, and Bali, she expanded and deepened her Soul's knowledge and true essence as a healer. For the last twelve years she has gathered immense experiences as a woman promoting sexual healing through Tantra and Energy therapy.

Leianna is working on her next book about her work as a sexual healer. She hopes to assist, enliven, and support anyone who seeks to celebrate a positive sexual identity, separate and apart from all notions of shame, guilt, and pornographic attitudes.

You can reach Leianna at
LeiannaLove@gmail.com

Feel free to seek her out, invite her in, and allow her to share what she does best.

References

<u>Free Form Conscious Dance:</u>

Gabrielle Roth, 5 Rhythms
www.5Rhythms.com

Lila Danielle, Beach Dance
www.BeachDance.com

Geordie Jahner Ph.D, Open Floor
www.OpenFloor.org

Samantha Sweetwater, Dancing Freedom
www.DancingFreedom.com

Amara Pagano, Azul and One Dance Tribe
www.AmaraPagano.com

Vinn Arjuna Marti, Soul Motion
www.SoulMotion.com

Somatic Psychology:

Naropa University
www.Naropa.edu

Bonnie Bainbridge Cohen
www.bodymindcentering.com

Janet Adler
www.disciplineofauthenticmovement.com

Matthew Fox
https://www.foxinstitute-cs.org

Spiritual Teachers:

Wayne Dyer
www.WayneDyer.com

Marianne Williamson
www.Marianne.com

Masaru Emoto
www.masaru-emoto.net/english/

Other:

Laura Lynne Dyer, Treehouse Wise Woman,
www.TheMagicLand.org

Joan Marie, Artist
www.JoanMarieArt.com

Kiesa Kay/ Author
www.amazon.com/Kiesa-Kay

Made in the USA
Middletown, DE
11 October 2022